beyond words

finding fulfillment

between the lines

this is a call to journal.

Michelle Bernard

Printed in the USA

ISBN

9781793077349

The author of this book does not prescribe the use of any technique or exercise as a form of treatment for physical, emotional, or medical problems without the advice of a physician or licensed therapist, either directly or indirectly. The information therein is of a general nature to help you in your quest for emotional, mental, and spiritual well-being. The author assumes no responsibility for your actions.

Michelle Bernard created the **black coffee journal series** for self-exploration and elevation.

offerings from Michelle Bernard

books.

Lean Happy Healthy You Book

Campout with the Lean Happy Healthy You Journal

JoG—LOSE WEIGHT, KEEP IT OFF, AND NEVER LOOK BACK—-this ain't no book about runnin'

journals.

the black coffee journals series—inspirational (mostly blank for writing) journals:

rise like fire

black coffee

37-ish Places I Can Be Myself

in your hands—28 days to connect with your Voice, expand your possibilities, and live above ordinary:

the journal complement to *beyond words—finding fulfillment between the lines*

courses.

the beyond words realness expedition

JoG to weight-loss and never look back

community.

Live Above Ordinary wellness, realness, and fulfillment community

www.liveaboveordinary.com

beyond words

finding fulfillment

between the lines

this is a call to journal.

for the
wild ones and human beans:
may you grow tall enough to see over
the brush.

contents

ink-stained 84

guideline three: set your shy pen free.

go beyond 126

guideline four: explore WiLD.

side note.

My initial title for this book was HOW TO START JOURNALING. Trumpets? No. Maybe violins. I dropped that boring title. Journaling has written me into so many of my aspirations, it still blows my mind. Through journaling I shaped the courage to move to the cities and into the careers I craved, despite what naysayers said about the economy, despite warnings that my desires were too outlandish to ask for. Because of journaling, I conquered my eating disorder and changed my relationship with food and my body. It's the reason I've been able to sustain my physical transformation for over twenty years. Time and again journaling has been the tool that's given me the Voice to declare and become the person I imagined. That tired title doesn't scratch the depths that journaling will reach. The title I chose does.

I'm definitely planning to show you *how* to journal. I'm gonna show you how to use your words to point yourself toward the experiences you desire. Your words are so powerful. They create. They destroy. They unlock, and they bind. Beyond your words awaits fulfillment. By journaling you will surely see how this is true.

I'll explain *why* journaling is the tool to improve your life. Yes, I said it. Journaling WILL IMPROVE your life. You will feel better. You will choose better. You will trust yourself more. You will declare with confidence. You will. I can't promise any hard or exact deadlines about how soon you'll see these improvements. A few sessions. One week. Three months. You're gonna arrive at your revelations, find your center, transcend your fear, summon brave momentum—all that stuff, whenever it happens to happen. But, know this—if you continue to journal daily, desirable changes are gonna happen.

Tools are used to fix things, so I hesitate to call journaling "a tool". It implies you are broken. So, think of a tool like the kind an artist uses. A sculptor uses a tool to carve, sand, and shine. Painters use tools to color, outline, and highlight what will become their masterpiece. You are that masterpiece the journal will outline, sand, highlight, color, and shine.

Daily journaling is gonna outline what you really want and sand away what you **really don't want**—anymore. Daily journaling will detox you from sour emotions before they can penetrate your body, zap your energy, or cause illness. Your journal will highlight your beliefs and help you reframe your fears; it will help you generate the fortitude to finish your projects and pursue the passions you've deferred. Your journal will delineate the direction you want your life to take. When you finish this book you'll understand why I reach for my pen, not my phone, first thing in the morning. Journaling is gonna elevate your life in ways Mark Zuckerberg hasn't thought of yet.

Another thing I "should" do every day, huh?

Is that what you're thinking? You already have an exhaustive should-do list. Me too. It's not fair for me to crowd another self-help task into your schedule unless it's worth it for you.

Is having more confidence, less confusion, more awareness, less doubt, and more focus on what matters to you, worth it? I agree. It is for me, also. You only need to set aside 10–25 minutes a day for all these jewels. You can do this.

Okay, one more thing. I did my darndest to keep this book short and to the point. I've included the essentials. I also kept the book short so you'll read the whole thing. You could probably knock it out in a week, but I suggest you trot through the book a bit slower. You'll absorb the benefits that way. There are four sections or guide*lines*, as I call them. The fourth guide*line* is super. Don't miss it. If you decide you want more guidance, you can go beyond this book with the **beyond words** online course (the realness expedition) and journal with me. I'll talk about that toward the end.

Ready? Give power to your beloved pen, and claim your page! This simple gesture is about to change your life.

the human bean:

a dedication

Besides the cafe in Silver Lake with the family-style wooden benches or Insomnia Cafe where I worked for a year, my favorite places to source inspiration were The Bodhi Tree Bookstore in Beverly Hills and Borders Books in Santa Monica. The smell of hardcovers at The Bodhi Tree competed with the Nag Champa burning behind the checkout counter, yum. The books sang to me there.

I'd visit the cafe below The Bodhi Tree where I'd either open my journal, read, or chat with strangers, including an occasional celeb. I said *hello* to singer, Randy Crawford, actress, Rae Dawn Chong, and "Newman" from SEINFELD. My actor bud and substitute teacher, Tovi, would hang with me. I often went alone. In a high-back chair with coffee by my side, I'd tell my life to my private book. Afterward, I'd head upstairs to The Bodhi Tree bookstore.

Yoga wasn't popular yet. I had a nutty-crunchy urge to "savasana" before it was mainstream. I'd run a finger down the spines of yoga and chakra books until one sang to me. Once I found my companion book, I'd plop onto the floor and become an afternoon student. I wasn't the only one. The incense and music lured most of the customers to camp on the floor for self-healing. I spotted Chaka Khan and Rhea Perlman listening for books in The Bodhi Tree. Chaka and Rhea in a New Age bookstore—not surprising.

It was 1995. I was 27. My Saturn was about to *Return*. You astrology connoisseurs understand what this means. If you don't follow the planets, just know I was desperately searching for some guidance. Fiction didn't give answers. In the late 90's, Self-Help books were being published in excess. Every week I'd graze them for messages.

The loft layout at Border's overwhelmed me. The books could breathe in that place and there were billions fighting for air. The "noise" of huffing and humming books clamored for my attention. I had to narrow my focus or take refuge in the bathroom.

Wayne Dyer's, **Real Magic**, had moved me. In one week I'd listened to the book twice on cassettes. I wanted more from Dyer—second floor. And there it was. SARK. Her name was hand-written in caps. I flipped the book over. SARK was an acronym for Susan Ariel Rainbow Kennedy. SARK. Did she make some of those names up, or was her mother that generous?

The cover was white with watercolor art like it'd been designed by a kid. The entire jacket was hand-written in black sharpie pen, right down to the publisher credits. *Inspiration Sandwich—Stories to Inspire Our Creative Freedom.*
Sounds like what I need.

I slid to the floor, set my coffee next to my purse, and with no care for time, started at page one. I forgot to mention that I was a starving artist doing one-woman shows with my guitarist. I also worked on-call for Universal Studios as the audience warm-up actor in The Rocky and Bullwinkle show and recorded demos when I wasn't serving coffee drinks at Insomnia. Sitting on bookstore floors, reading for free, was a lucky perk that fit sweetly into my lifestyle.

I read the whole thing that day. The interior was written in black pen like a journal, every bit by hand, not typed like a regular book. On a few pages she used colorful magic markers. *Inspiration Sandwich* sung like child's play, but the entries spoke of daring, grown-up adventures.

SARK told me her secrets. She asked herself questions, then answered them and let me in on the whole conversation. She wasn't afraid of appearing complicated. Or brave. Or odd. Or brilliant. She wasn't ashamed of being scared. She admitted her stumbles and gave props to curiosity for shaping her destiny.

SARK, a lifelong adventurer, risk-taker, questioner, truth-teller, seeker; had published her personal diary! Her book looked like the journal in my purse. I was holding a mirror. I was holding my permission slip.

SARK has authored 16 books as I write this, most of them journal-like. Succulent Wild Woman, The Bodacious Book of Succulence, and Transformation Soup are my prize possessions. A few months later when I moved to New York, I attended her workshop. Her talk was held in a space no bigger than a grade school classroom. I sat close enough to see her cuticles. We all sat close to her. SARK was a real person, a woman with a human body, human hair, human hands, and a human laugh. She was a real **human bean**—as she often calls herself. And she did not refrain from appearing amazing and flawed, frozen and baffled, hurt, weird, or wild in real life. She signed my copy of Succulent Wild Woman that night. I floated away from her workshop like a giddy eleven-year-old, surrounded by bubbles of inspiration and driven to fulfill my ideas, no matter what.

The memories of reading the SARK ~~books~~ journals (I have read ten of them—and I dip back into my three favorites every year) are juicy and sweet. Her journals have been my therapists, kindreds, messengers, and muses.

This book, **beyond words,** is dedicated to my magic wand, SARK. She's not responsible for starting my journaling practice. But happening upon *Inspiration Sandwich* felt like a divine wink, a subtle nudge to listen to my life, to pay attention, and to declare my truth because it would lead me exactly where I wanted to go.

Thank you for your marvelous messaging, SARK. You'll be delighted to know I have become ever so succulent, bodacious, and WiLD.

From Buunni Cafe
Bronx, New York
On a hot summer day (the way I like 'em) of 2018

foreword.

It was the summer of 2003. A group of future teachers sat stuffed into a tiny classroom. It was hot and humid—and everyone looked wide-eyed and nervous. We had no idea what we were doing or about to do, yet we all gathered as a cohort from the NYC Teaching Fellows Program. We were future teachers, hell-bent on changing the lives of children.

In our first class of the program, there sat Michelle. Something about Michelle caught my attention immediately. She was so alive. She was so passionate—she exuded a magical air. I had to be friends with her. Like a young high school student, I would save her a seat everyday, hoping she'd sit next to me; but she would always choose a seat closest to the door. Turns out she was running out to meet her boyfriend!

A few weeks passed, and our cohort traveled to the Metropolitan Museum of Art. We all sat on the steps discussing our summer placements and issues as new teachers. It was at this moment that we had the chance to connect—and I was smitten. Having only spoken about education and our masters program {so far}, Michelle was quick to open up about life, love, success, and her dreams. We became instant friends and realized we shared the same opinions and visions about life. We both believed strongly in the power of intention. She told me how she visualized her dreams into being. She shared a glimpse of her journal—a huge juicy notebook filled with writing, calendars, and art. She told me this was how she created the life she wanted to live. I too had been a lifelong journaler—it was here that we realized we were meant to be.

Our relationship would grow through the years as we suffered through our first years of teaching and managing life in NYC. In addition to talking on the phone EVERY NIGHT (yes, this is true), we would meet at a cafe in the West Village and write our graduate school papers together. Her intensity and motivation always impressed me. Together we were a force, inspiring one another to write these long graduate school papers. As our friendship grew through the years—Michelle remained a trustworthy, positive sounding-board for my life and career.

Michelle would go on to be a bridesmaid at my wedding and witness the birth of my children. While we have many things in common, our strongest shared interest is our love of journaling and planning out our dreams. In between our graduate essays, we would journal and plan—I would write point by point the life I wanted to live, with Michelle mindfully rounding out my dreams. We would always site and refer to our shared idol—SARK, who wrote passionately about living and loving life. And to me, Michelle was my own SARK—inspirational, quirky, and always dreaming. If anyone can make their dreams come true—it's Michelle—one of the most confident, kind, thoughtful, inspiring humans with a heart full of love for everyone.

Lauren Juceam, MS Ed
June 2018

journaling surpasses other modes of self-exploration. the journal lets you witness
then save your Self in a container you can reference at any time.
the information you discover strengthens your bond with your Self.

the f-word.

Are you happy?

That question used to irritate me.

Me. *Well, what do you mean?*

I'd stammer.

Me again. *Right now? In this moment? At work? With myself? In life? WHAT DO YOU MEAN?*

Are You Happy? broke my concentration. *I was okay a minute ago. I was doing fine before you pushed me to come up with an answer to that loaded question.*

Are You Happy? set me to thinking about the stuff I'd shoved down.

Oh man. I was doing fine suppressing my anger and disappointment toward... mama, daddy, high school, the decision to eat that whole loaf of pumpkin bread and sleep with Paul again.

Are You Happy? made me wish for a more reasonable question to answer like *Are You Busy? Are You Hungry? Are You Coming? Are You Sleepy?*

Are You Happy? reminded me that, for some unclear reason, I wasn't.

This was until about five years ago. I'm as happy as box of chocolates these days. I never know what I'm gonna get, but I'm sure it'll be close, if not exactly match the pictures I focus on in my imagination.

When I was regularly **not happy**, I made sure no one could tell. One might wonder, based on the way my life looked back then, why the *happy* question irked me so. My journey has been pretty magical and willful. I've followed dreams wide and deep. I've taken risks that opened doors to my goals year upon year. I've been able to set up lives in each of the cities I dreamed about since childhood like Chicago, Los Angeles, Manhattan; and for a short time, Osaka, Japan. Paris and Costa Rica are written into future dream bubbles—my journal is making those plans. I've bypassed the traditional protocol to rise into the jobs I've wanted, often appointed because the people who hired me thought I was so enthusiastically happy. Hmmm?! Where the heck was my missing peace? (Deliberate spelling.)

I was a stage performer as a kid, an animated child you didn't have to direct or coax into getting prepared. I could learn a new song in a matter of minutes. I'd convey them with feeling before I was old enough to understand what the lyrics meant. I picked Barbra Streisand, Donna Summer, Diana Ross, and Cher to emulate and rarely compared myself to my peers. I was never shy about entertaining audiences. I'd assemble them anyway I could. During winter recess in sixth grade, I'd gather bodies on the playground to sit in the snow and watch my concerts.

Throughout high school and college I collected opportunities, awards, and fans for my talent. Yep, the accolades made me happy; so happy, it often perplexed others.

"Michelle! God, girl! Why the hell are you smiling?", a friend blurted out as I stepped onto the campus bus at The University of Iowa.

I was a sophomore. I knew so many people I had to squint to see who was asking the question. I sat next to CeCe. *Am I smiling?*

"Yes. You got on the bus smiling."

Really... I did? I don't know. I guess I smile a lot.

I did—I smiled all the time. People asked me about it all the time, too. Of course I'd answer: *Really... I am? I guess I smile a lot.*

My life was fulfilling—I was a sought-after soloist that gigged with different bands every weekend. I had a friend no matter where I turned, my dude loved me, and I was, for sure, on my way to a blissful future of more of the same. Traveling the world giving music; that was my plan, and I was on track to live among stars.

Even Sally saw it. Sally was my English professor, a quirky white lady with a big ole blonde, halo afro. She let us lounge on the classroom floor while she read poetry. Sally expressed passion for classical poetry the same way I felt songs. But looking up at Sally, I hardly heard the poems she read. Sally glistened. Sally shimmered. She floated above the words. Rode unicorns over the stanzas. All I could hear was her vibration. I imagined Sally's future—an Ivy-league graduate typing her novels by fireside in her chic and shabby Woodstock cottage. I was distracted by her fashionably tattered scarves, frayed kimonos, wrinkled gauchos, and ripped leggings.

I saw Sally. I saw myself.

Before I disappeared on the last day of the semestre, Sally called me over—*Michelle, you have stars all around you. I see them. Twinkling. All around you. Do you know that?* She smiled into my smile. I believed her.

Lifted by constant praise and a love for my life, I knew I had those stars around me—till I developed vocal problems during my last year of college.

My voice. My voice. The music. Stopped. To fill the silence I closed my eyes and stomped toward graduation. It was high time I imagined reality, grew up, and got serious. That was pretty much when happiness pulled away.

I only know **happy** disappeared then, because I was journaling when it left. I journaled before it left. I journaled after it left. If I hadn't been tracking the loss of my voice, I would have misread my dialed down joy as basic frustration over the break-up with my boyfriend. I lost one of those that same year.

I wrote myself into a new story. A new choice; less lyrical, less musical, less... magical. Less me. More like the me I was, maybe, supposed to be. Everything happens for a reason, right? I searched for that reason but kept returning to—*pursue a real job, girl, and get on with it,* which was the same as hearing *just shut up, keep your head down, and grow up.*

I'll be fine, I thought. If I put my head down and keep moving, I will be fine.

vocal repair.

Why did this happen to me? Did I do something wrong? I'd try to shake the questions, biting my tongue to avoid getting angry about my missing peace. *Things will work out fine,* I reminded myself.

I wanted to appear unblemished. If I spoke my sour feelings out loud, I'd look like I'd lost control. Like a hot-mess. I wanted to be thought of as patient and spiritual. *This too shall pass*; I memorized those words just so I could swallow *fine* without gagging.

I stuffed down anxiety about my future. Frustration with God put a bad taste in my mouth. I wished I had the nerve to tell Life and the Universe what I ~~wanted~~ needed. I wanted to scream at the world, myself, and God for rupturing my music and love relationships and handing me unshakable issues with my weight. When I couldn't deflect any more anger, I went to my journal and ~~spoke~~ expelled an unladylike tirade. I needed someone... something to hear my truth.

I lost my voice in my early twenties.
But, I've gotten it back.

You're gonna understand how as we roll along, though here's a hint—whispering ➡ the journal brought it back. I use my Voice all the time now. My Interior Voice. I listen and learn from it. Using my journal has changed how I show up in the world and how the world shows up for me. Whether you need to recover something or activate something in your life, the same can happen for you. If you are willing to listen to your Voice using your journal, it will.

Now is a good time to tell you, I don't stock my satchel with small talk. Surface conversation makes me feel like I'm speaking as a surrogate for Michelle. 'You okay with transparency? Because I'm gonna express how I feel and how I've felt, and *fine* has never been a fit answer for me. Inspirational speaker, Mel Robbins, calls *fine* the f-word. When I used to say *I'm fine*, I was not acknowledging my real state of mind or body, even to myself.

I'm not in resistance to myself anymore. I plan to be forthright with you like I am with my journal. I'll be sharing some personal deets throughout guide*line* one. I had second thoughts about how personal, but what the heck.... It'll be useful. I hope my personal stories help you unveil yours. I hope that as I express who I've been and who I'm becoming, it'll give you permission to express what you feel now and declare what you really want to feel and experience in your life from now on. I know I'm dropping a lot of **hope** on you, but soon all this *hope* will deliver as promised. I'm counting on it.

You and I are going to journal together, go beyond words together, discover and declare together. Which reminds me to ask: Do you have a journal? You'll need blank pages and something to write with. We'll answer questions, overcome resistance, and move through difficult emotions. You will write yourself into the life you desire.

Excited? Me too. It'll be epic. (New school EPIC, not Odyssey EPIC). I've been known for being *dramatic*. The rumors are true. I'm not exaggerating here, though.

Stay calm, Michelle. They're just getting to know you.

You too. Stay calm. Wipe the sweat from your nose. I won't make you wait till guide*line* four to start journaling. There are conversation starters (journaling questions) sprinkled throughout **beyond words** so you can get your self-discovery on right away. You can journal using all the conversation starters in the **hands are for...** sections, or skip a conversation starter and return to it later. The way to fulfillment is in your hands. Literally.

Let's be honest, we have a lot in common. We want to be successful at forming and maintaining relationships. We want to choose a meaningful career path. We endeavor to raise interesting children. Good health and having plenty of money to do the things we love are resolutions we jot down every year. Plus, we want to feel protected and loved by somebody in the world. By the way, if none of these things appeal to you or none of these things need to be improved in your life, then... well... hmmm... you might be blemish-free after all. If you're without any needs or desires, you'd probably benefit from journaling about *disillusionment*.

We all aim to get our needs met. This is why we have goals, dreams, bucket lists, desires. They give our lives purpose. Goals challenge us to grow. For all human beans, growth is why we were planted here!

What do you want? What would make you feel fulfilled? What is your **happy**?

Think of one of your goals right now. That goal will either get ushered into your reality or buried in darkness. It depends on your personal thoughts and beliefs about that goal. Of course, you hope your thoughts and beliefs are supporting you to reach your goal. But, what if they aren't? Maybe you have no clue whether your thoughts are supporting or sabotaging you. Most of your thoughts and beliefs are beneath the surface of your awareness. During guide*line* two, **tell the truth,** you'll learn how journaling lets you see beneath your surface. Journaling exposes exactly what's holding you away from fulfillment and what's mapping you straight toward it. Guide*line* three, **set your shy pen free,** introduces you to WiLD, my foundational journaling practice. You'll learn the fundamentals of journaling for 10–25 minutes each day. There are journaling rules that you'll follow rebelliously—by breaking them. Guide*line* four, **explore WiLD,** is special. You'll use the seven journaling practices that brought back the stars to my life. These practices helped me overcome doubt, detox from stress and worry, forgive aspects of my past, and get clear about who I aim to be.

Living fulfilled is like riding waves. Waves vary. Some are high and mighty, some uneventful, and some break. We keep looking to catch a good one. There is something worthy to discover no matter what kind of wave we catch. The seven offerings in guide*line* four let you witness your life, whether it's riding high or low, and still find fulfillment.

A few suggestions before we begin: Be straight-forward. Tell your story to your journal without a chaser. Your journal can handle it. There's information behind your words. At this very moment, your dominant thoughts are actively shaping your life. So write everything;

every thought and every feeling, even the ugly ones. Don't judge yourself for what you're thinking. Don't hide. Just write. Over time, your journal will show you what you can shift, step away from, challenge, or celebrate.

Here I go **hoping** again. I hope you'll see how wise you are because of your journal. I hope you'll reach farther into your imagination because of your journal. I hope you'll believe in more possibilities than you did before. Tall order? Yep. Drink it up. It'll nourish you.

Besides, it's possible you could live till you're 112 years old.
How do you expect to stay busy for all those years? Watching Netflix and playing lotto?
Might as well do something liberating and be who you really are. I mean—be happy.

hands are for... listening

◎ **What would you like to receive, learn, or understand about yourself by journaling?**

There are things we don't want others to know about us. I did not want anyone to know I was not as patient, spiritual, and unblemished as I appeared.

◎ **What are you hiding from others?**
Write *I DON'T WANT PEOPLE TO KNOW THAT I_____(and fill in the blank).*
Write as many of these as you want.

◎ **How would you feel if after you revealed the things you've been trying to hide, you were accepted, respected, and loved anyway?**

There is no greater agony
than bearing an untold story inside you.

MAYA ANGELOU

know thyself

spend a morning in the wild.
your journal can get you there.
the wild,
where first is revealed
a dense, chaotic territory.
prickly vines
waxy
layers of feeling
a tapestry of
brush unexamined by eyes
or ears
or pens.

stay this morning.
give the journal
your wild.
cross over thatch and leaves and other matters
of being
with your pen
and a warm drink

go beyond
what you can see
with just
your eyes.

guide*line* one : become a witness.

who are you? who do you want to be? what fulfills you?
look into yourself to know.
when you know who you are, no matter what happens,
you understand that the patterns of your life have a purpose.

morning.

It's cold. I need to walk with something warm next to my gloves—something comfortable, something familiar. I choose coffee.

A paper cup of freshly steeped espresso with a crown is the comfort I prefer. I order my cappuccino to-go, though I am eager for a taste as soon as I have it in my hand.

The nutty aroma rises as I pinch the lid off. Raw sugar granules sink into the cinnamon creating brown tunnels. I don't dump the entire pack of sugar in; something I've been practicing as a health and fitness coach—a habit that quelled my sweet tooth. Just two-thirds of the pack goes in. Plenty sweet.

This morning I am somewhat patient. I must wait or the coffee will burn my tongue. I can tell because my gloves are warm. I gently blow into the foam.

The first and second sips are frothy. The next, as I leave the cafe and head into New York's gray January wind, is complex; espresso rich. I secure the lid before I walk down the subway stairs.

A breeze. My train is coming. Not to risk spilling what's left, I carefully slide the metro card with my free hand and bump the turnstile with my hip.

The end seat is available. A little bit of elbow-room. I feel lucky whenever there's a seat on the train. I remove the lid and slurp the rest of my comfort. Tastes like morning.

I use the napkin to absorb the last drops, then smash the cup into my bag. I feel around for my journal. It's saved in Evernote on my iPad—easier to journal with my "Pad" when commuting to work.

I type my morning thoughts, yesterday's bumps, and today's wonderings. Sometimes I journal a daydream. Sometimes I hover around my fears with questions. Sometimes I write the answers. I tell everything to my journal. My dear ole diary. My dear ole friend.

While I'm writing in the journal, nothing else exists. I don't care that the guy in the corner seat with headphones is rapping out loud. I don't pay attention to the clump of people in the middle aisle swaying and breathing in each other's backpacks and hair conditioner. I don't hear the automated "lady voice" when it announces my stop.

Surprisingly, I've only missed my stop once while journaling. I've programmed the forty minute commute, so my body knows when to pull attention from typing and get up.

On this day, I barely make it out the subway doors before they close.

Journaling is a part of my morning ritual and it has been for four solid years. I used to write in my journal during my morning commute. Same routine every day. Coffee, train, lucky seat, iPad, write.

That was two years ago.

These days I journal at home. I wake and walk the dogs. Afterward, I pour a goblet of iced coffee and sit near my window to write. My ritual. My morning routine.

If my journaling time gets compromised, my day feels off. Last winter a client needed an early morning exercise session for two weeks straight. Since it interfered with my ritual, I took my journal to work and wrote for 15 minutes during a coffee break. My morning routine positions me for the telling, listening, feeling, and awakening that happens when I speak in my private book.

what you write on the pages reveals your mind.
*you'll discover your **will** and your **won't,** your desire and your disdain.*
you'll witness your excuses and your landslides.
I used to journal only when I felt lost. now that I journal every day,
I never feel separated from my true Self. I never feel disoriented when the darkness hovers.
the journal shows me where I am light.

lost and found.

A year before I published my first book about fitness, I took an online writing course to juice my creativity. I had plenty of extra time. I was newly married, newly living in a house in Central Jersey, and freshly separated from my rent-stabilized Manhattan dwelling. White-knuckling my New York life, I kept my clients in The City. This spelled out a third commitment: L-O-N-G C-O-M-M-U-T-E. It took me nearly two hours to travel into Uptown Manhattan for work. Luckily I was able to fit all my personal training clients into three days instead of five. Those three days started early.

Had I inflicted some kind of torture on myself, erecting a schedule that required multiple train rides at the crack of dawn?

Why don't you let go of The City and get clients in New Jersey, Michelle?, something whispered.

Not just yet, something else answered.

I had to wake by 4:30 am to make the 5:30 train into The City. The raised eyebrows and crinkled foreheads taking pity on me were too many to count.

How long does it take you to get here, Michelle?

Oh wow. Aren't you tired?

4:30! What time do you have to go to bed?

Ah, that's not gonna work. You're gonna get fed up with it.

Sure. People were right to question my decision. But my early train ride bestowed a gift.

Three mornings a week I had a few choices.

1. Sleep my way into Manhattan
2. Tumble down the rabbit hole. You know... Facebook.
3. Answer my creative curiosity.

I dipped into each, but one stuck. As much as I loved to absorb self-help books, I leaned into my infatuation with Gillian Flynn novels. I finished *Gone Girl* in my backyard but consumed the rest of her catalog, plus other books, during those train rides.

Where else was I gonna get a 4-hour block to read (and finish) a book?

I finished a book every month on those train rides.

Write Yourself Alive was the writing course I mentioned earlier. It was organized by Andrea Balt of Rebelle Society, the online magazine I wanted to get published in. The five-week course prompted me to write from a series of questions that explored authenticity and the creative process—journal style.

Who wouldn't be thrilled to have time to enroll and actually finish ALL the assignments in an online writing course?

Three days a week I dumped the assignments along with random thoughts and feelings into Evernote on my iPad. On weekends, I'd write in the online forum. After five consecutive weeks of journaling on the train and at home, I was hooked and writing every day. Two months after the course ended I pieced together an essay from several journal entries. It got published on the Rebelle Society platform, my first published article ever. Yes! Nine months later, I finished my first book, *Lean Happy Healthy You*. Yes, yes! The *Write Yourself Alive* course was the taster that got me craving journaling—again.

I have returned to New York. Living and working. In the Bronx this time. No train commute anymore; I walk to all my clients. No husband either. That was a ~~happy~~ satisfactory ending for both of us. I gave the details of that story to my girlfriends so this book wouldn't end up being about how to journal through ex-boyfriends and a husband.

New York City life equals hectic days. Seven days a week I rush to clients, teach classes, write blog posts, and make fitness and yoga videos. New Jersey life gave me two straight years of journaling freedom because of the long-ass commute. When the writing space on the train came to an end, I felt I'd lost my touchstone to emotional grounding. My journal kept me aware and decisive. My journal listened when I vented, applauded when I won. My journal let me stir ideas, bitch in secret, and blow dreams into bubbles. When I needed to be transported away from my current reality, I would rise up into those bubbles. Journaling on the train was an escape from confusion into the epicenter of answers. One week after returning to New York, and I was itching to check-in with my dear old friend. When would we speak again? Same as before, I decided. In the morning.

Later to sleeping in. Better to stay awake.

My alarm clock breathes and pants. It's my goofy chocolate Lab, Professor; Prof—for short. Picture Scooby Doo licking your nostril at 5:15 in the morn, then shaking his booty, which, because of his size, shakes the whole bed. I'm up. (Because of Prof, I can never sleep in).

I journal at home now. It begins by 6:30 every morning of every week. Without fail, I walk Mr. Porter, my creme and tan Shih Tzu with the face of Mr. Peabody (you might have to google that one), and Prof. After, I remove their leashes, fill a goblet with iced coffee, add Irish Cream flavored creamer; then burrow near the window with an easy pen, lamp light, and a view of... well... a big rock and a few trees! Exceptional. It's the Bronx.

I sip sweet coffee and gaze out the window for a few minutes—breathing, thinking, but kinda in slow motion. Squirrels and birds collect discarded trash, food, and leaves. It's summertime right now. My view will be green for three months. There are a few lucky trees that haven't gotten plowed. The City is building a new complex in the lot behind mine—another apartment in New York, good-bye nature. Most days it's quiet at this time, except for those birds, squirrels, and the stray cats three stories down in the small backyard. People aren't active. No one's using voices yet. I write. Nature is my soundtrack. My Voice is the lead, and it's loud and present through my pen.

I never, ever have to search for something to say to my journal. There's yesterday to remember. There's tomorrow to wonder about. There are dreams to etch into bubbles. There are conflicts to peel back and possibilities to ponder. I have thoughts that are better written before they're spoken. I have feelings to set free, to neutralize, to transmute.

I write like I'm talking to someone; someone who is me but She is an extraordinary listener, quiet and accepting, letting me press all my stuff through the pen before responding. And I tend to be patient as She responds. This is different from my real-life tendency. In real conversation, I've been called out for jumping in with advice before the speaker is done with the story. I don't like that I do that. To my journal, I never do that.

Something in me was pulled to journal way before I memorized Julia Cameron's order. She assigned morning pages in her book, *The Artist's Way*. At age 26, morning pages held my hand for the two years I lived on LaBrea and Franklin in Hollywood. Saturn had definitely *Returned* to rule my galaxy. I wondered if I'd make it back to Earth without becoming permanently spaced-out and apathetic.

When J. Cameron's, *The Artist's Way,* came out entertainers followed it like a roadmap. We did our morning pages because J.C. said *do your morning pages.* Free-write. Three pages.

Every day. Check. I filled two 5-subject notebooks, the first one red, the second blue. I sat at my kitchen's only window with a coffee doing my duty. I needed to write those pages just to de-clutter my crowded head.

I'd write at 10 or 11 every morning. (I considered 11 am *morning* when I was 26).
I loved them. I needed them. They showed me what to do next. Those pages were fingers, eyes, and ears. They gave me the first, close-up look at my Saboteur—a scaly, jagged-toothed Troll, no a Gnome. A Gnome is a sinister little creature whose mission is to shield your personal treasures. His idea of *shielding* meant **he'd suppress my treasures**. Yep, he's my Gnome. A Gnome with light eyes, up-turned at the corners, tiny feet, and three bumpy toes. While I'd journal, he'd unpack enough hogwash about my relationships and daddy to fill a trough, then he'd slop it across my mind.

- *Awww, Michelle. That guy you're smitten by is **not** gonna do what he says. You'll see.*
- *Men. They're all the same, Michelle. Can't be trusted. You're such a fool.*
- *Come on, you know he's gonna cheat on you!*
- *You don't actually believe **you** deserve all that silly stuff you want, do you?*
- *What makes you so special?*
- *They are **all** gonna disappoint you. You're so stupid.*

He'd snarl and roll his eyes at my childhood dreams.

- *You're so dramatic.*
- *You think too much.*
- *You want too much.*
- *You are too much.*

- *Get real and quit checking on those bubbles.*
- *Pop those bubbles of dreams and grow up. You're not 12 anymore.*

These were his favorite things to say to me. Still are, when I think of it.

My Gnome expressed doubt in me, while my Child Self handed me Her fantasies. I saved both the disses and the fantasies in my morning pages and later turned them into art. Those spiral notebooks inspired the poems and songs I performed in cafe concerts and on demos. Within a few months of moving to New York, I entered a poetry slam at the famous Nuyorican Poet's Cafe in the East Village and won. I had so much content in my journals, I hardly had to prepare.

Thank you, Julia Cameron. You were right. Dumping three pages at the top of the day really does relieve emotional constipation. Those pages supported my dreams to perform, to change cities, and to change my career. Creation can exist amidst destruction. Both will share space on your page. Journaling every day has helped me tell one from the other.

hands are for... listening

◎ **What have you wanted to experience or accomplish but can't find the time to start or complete?**

◎ **Why does it matter to you?**

◎ **How would your life change if you started or completed it?**

climbing yesterday.

sutures of creativity
grief
bravery
longing
music
triumph
stitched into my book.

mountains of experience.

peaks made from memories,
marking a life.

messy memories.

who hasn't got a gnarly stash of 'em?

In the past, I mainly journaled to navigate challenges. By challenges, I mean relationships. After graduation, I cried on a yellow legal pad as my first grown-up "love" dissolved. We'd moved in together. The skid from college and its comforts (including a social conglomerate of which I sat high on the pyramid) down to adulthood, gave me diaper burn. To assimilate I charged a pair of khakis and a full-sized futon with the Discover card I had no way to pay off, and I clocked in with the rest of the grown folks. I'd moved to Chicago to follow destiny which was supposed to include bright light, big city realness and a forever bond with my dude. Instead, I nestled into the only stable relationship within reach: the one with my journal.

How many ways could my pen write *disappointed*? My journal knew them all. Heartsick over my "roommate" plus contempt for my soulless job forced my lips into a permanent frown. On weekends when I wasn't taking a 12-hour nap or eating, I'd scribble *why and WTF* over the legal pad. Because of good time-management, I'd usually squeeze in equal parts of all three. Eventually my roomie ~~boyfriend~~ resurrected his bed back at his mama's house. I was left to plummet into the deep blue futon abyss—alone, pissed, and puzzled.

I was living and working full-time in the big city, wasn't I? Wasn't this one of my dream bubbles? I'd gotten *some* of what I asked for plus some of what I didn't, like withdrawal symptoms over losing boundless friends and a rapidly thickening waist and hip circumference. With tubes of room temperature cookie dough to keep me company (I don't think salmonella poisoning actually exists) and a Sade record on repeat, I entered into Saturday night staring contests. Eyes on the phone, then the wall, then the phone again. Twenty-two years in Eastern Iowa had not prepared me for the reality I was experiencing. Why were people so eager to become adults? My inner Voice groveled when I wrote about this in my journal. *Toughen up, girl.* The Voice said. *Organize a city attitude. Go hang out in coffee shops like you did in school.*

Plop me in any city, anywhere on a map, and in three weeks I can tell you where the coolest cafes are. In that LA cafe under The Bodhi Tree bookstore I wrote myself into and out of a romance with an older man who had four Emmys and a casual habit with cocaine and pot. Doma Cafe in Greenwich Village felt like Italy. I'd dedicate twenty minutes of journaling to exorcise my real-life Gnome, Phil, who was my Italian lover and ex-boss. Afterward, I would slog through first drafts of college papers with Lauren who wrote the foreword to this book. Oh, then there's Max Cafe. I wrote half this book there. I journaled at Max more than any other cafe in New York City. Journaling at Max got me through two other romances—one weird and one amazing, and... Let me stop right here to ease your mind again: this is not a book about the best cafes across the country nor is it about how to get over your exes. It's just that my journals were bridges over those kinds of challenges. Journaling handed me an understanding of why I choose certain relationships. You know what else I want to tell you? Journaling about my lovers in cafes fared safer for me. Seriously, how much cursing or crying could I get away with on a public sofa?

The journal has been a mirror. Regarding relationships, my journal revealed what I was allowing and what I was blocking. The entries reflected what I *really* thought beneath my surface. I was uninspired by the concept of marriage. During adolescence, I lacked faith in the *forever* scenario. I considered marriage a fairy tale. I didn't believe *forever love* was real.

I never journaled about my wedding or imagined the perfect dress. I didn't cry when tin cans rattled from car bumpers. I gave my pen and imagination to romance. I dreamed of having conversations on the terrace at sunset, sharing dinners in cozy restaurants, singing and playing games during long car rides. I wrote about these things as much I wrote about my distrust of matrimony. Connection, romance, and friendship were my ideas of relationship bliss. The things I wanted and the things I feared about relationships, I experienced in real-life. It ~~was~~ is common for my exes to call years after the break-up to chat, be friendly, and ask me out for cozy dinners. It made sense that I kept becoming buddies ever-after with my long-term boyfriends.

This pattern matched the decision I'd made unconsciously, a belief I'd programmed unknowingly. I manifested the kinds of relationships I was available to receive. If I wanted to manifest a life-long bond or a lasting marriage, I would have to imagine, decide, declare, and believe in one. I'm doing that now in my journal.

Okay, what I just told you about my relationship imprint is a recent revelation. My journal exposed my contradictions to love while I was writing this book. I can envision and declare the kind of love I desire, now. Right there... another reason why I'm happy today, and another reason why I journal every day.

confronting an unsupportive belief right now, a belief that has kept me from having
the life I imagine.
I wrote about it for 25 minutes this morning. my WiLD Tomato entry.
gonna keep looking at it, questioning it, and dismantling it all week.
glad I have a place where I can do this privately.

never again.

My first "journal" was a pink diary with a paisley print cover and a silver lock. I found it at Woolworth's and paid for it with my allowance. I'm pretty sure the Judy Blume book I read in fourth grade inspired me to get it. I had just learned cursive, which I hear they don't teach anymore—sad. It's so pretty. Anyway, I couldn't wait to swirl words over those pages. I'd write before bed, say my prayers, then push my pink diary between my mattress and bedspring for safe hiding. After two months, that diary was found and read. It wasn't locked. I'd lost both keys. I didn't write in that pink diary after that.

By middle school, I was forced to journal for Drama class. It was the first activity assigned before we did acting exercises. The class was allowed to sit anywhere we wanted in the auditorium for 15 minutes of free-writing. I hated it. I'd look around to see if anyone else was as empty as I was. Like the character "Morales" in *A Chorus Line*, I felt nothing when it was time to write. Mostly, I feared someone like my teacher, or God-forbid, a student in class would read my feelings if I left them bare and exposed in that stupid journal. For a good grade I wrote stuff I knew my teacher wanted to hear. It was a bunch of mess with no depth or personal meaning. I got an A in Drama.

A few years later, I had too much to say. My high school diaries read like the Facebook posts you never want your employer to see. I groped for an outlet to voice my discoveries. Hormones were responsible. I'm sure of it. Or maybe it was the experimental drug use and alcohol. Surely, it had something to do with boys. Or having to negotiate my way around cliques. I have no idea how a kid survives high school without a private book to speak to. My journals got a lot of noise after weekend parties when I smelled of green plants and cheap beer. I'd write till I feel asleep. I wrote to quell my yearning to leave Iowa. I wrote about my future in the big city where I'd find peace on stages, in costumes, behind songs.

By age 16, I craved paper. I'd turn any book with blank space into a journal. The black and white composition booklet I was supposed to use for Science class: a journal. Extra long legal pads: journals. My dad's half-used ledger even became a journal. Spiral notebooks, loose leaf scraps, and napkins worked too. I'd stuff those loose paper entries into Prince and Donna Summer album jackets. No one would think to spy for them there. My private books contained song lyrics I'd dissected to find their true meanings. I described my future life in Los Angeles where I knew I'd bump around with movie producers and record moguls. I wrote about my forbidden love with Gregg, the white boy with a bigoted father. He became the muse for pages of poetry dripped in passion and agony. I got to tell Gregg that he'd been the star of my high school diary when we spent weeks together in New York thirty years later. I'm grateful I stored those memories in private books.

Those old high school journals await my return. They sit in "Michelle" boxes in my mom's basement. I can only hope they're undisturbed. They must be, because if my mother knew about my youthful shenanigans, she'd immediately schedule counsel with a preacher to repent for blind-sighted mothering. It's not her fault I was curious about sex, drugs, and rock'n roll. Blame it on Elvis or Michael Jackson. I mean Prince. Yes, Prince made me that way. Seriously. He did.

I specifically remember not keeping a journal during my first years of college. I took my happy smile and bubbles of dreams to The University of Iowa. That road was paved with fame, friendship, and weekend festivities. I never slowed down to look inward or reflect. I didn't feel like I needed to. I had stars around me. Fast, blinking stars.

Then, I lost my Voice. I was a semester away from graduating. I was also a bit chubbier, with a bit more forehead acne, a bit more anxiety, and in full denial about my anger. My boyfriend lived in another city and we were doing what 21 year-olds do when they're unsure about the relationship. Experimenting. My body was better looking under baggy clothes. I was losing and gaining the wrong things. Adding **resignation** to my repertoire, I wrote resumes and random journal entries to prepare for graduation.

Within a week of graduating, I packed my fragile relationship along with whatever could fit in my rental car and moved to Chicago's westside. I resumed sporadic journaling when I got settled there. I had to.

It was dizzying, the way my life came to a screeching halt. No one properly positions young folks for a smooth entry into the after-life called adulthood. Probably because it is a kind of death. You're catapulted out of a twenty year nursery of school assignments, rewards, and playtime into... **stagnation**, I mean "a job". If you leave your hometown, you have to recover from a different whiplash. You leave behind 500 girlfriends, cheap places to party, and options to sleep-in. No one's looking at you in the hallway anymore. No one's sending money to pay your bills. No one's trying to flirt with you while you order your morning croissant. In a new city doing daily stagnation to earn your keep, every day feels like the first day of summer camp—*who will sit with me, who will hang with me, who will **get** me, does anybody want to have fun, who will be my friend?*

I *had* to journal to get through the "first day of camp" experience.

Stagnation turned into fermentation. I ended up burying my rotted relationship, keeping for myself the full rent slip and two friends, one with a kid she adored more than her husband, one who dated a married man who also had a kid; and unrelenting heart-burn. This made for journal entries that were sour and smelled of resentment. And lengthy! Ah, the wreckage of brooding tears. For a whole year I sulked on the page. And the great mistake: I re-read that sappy dribble. Ugh! I was becoming my version of Billie Holiday.

Enough.

I ripped a handful of those pages off the spine and stomped them into my garbage. As I write this, I remember promising to NEVER KEEP A JOURNAL AGAIN. Use an English accent for *AGAIN* when you read it. That's how I heard the word in my mind.

my journals keep making me cry.

[Background music: a Toni Braxton song from the 90s.]

AGAIN, I vowed to stop keeping journals. How could I thrive if I continued to record sad, depressing catalogs of my life?

DO NOT re-read your journal entries right away if they are depressing. What qualifies as depressing? If you have to ask, you're probably not going through a depressing time. When you are depressed, melancholy, apathetic, and resentful your entries sound really hopeless, really sad, really angry, and really fed-up for weeks upon weeks! And the pages themselves might be crinkled from dried tears.
Been there? Most folks who journal have.

During the blues, handle your journal like this:
Keep writing your heart out, friend. Tell the truth on those pages. It's good for you.
Discharging angst and bitterness is cathartic. Travel through your darkness on paper. It will lead you to a brighter side in real-life.

However, my friend, **do not re-read those entries until you get way past your pain**.
If you re-read too soon, it'll give your nightmare surround sound.

As a practice, I re-read some of my journal entries one or two months after I've written them.

I usually wait longer. **My collection of depressing journal entries, however, remain unseen until I'm at least six months to one year away from the pain.** I wait till I'm fully resolved before I re-see them. Or, I ball the pages up, toss 'em into the trash and pour hot bacon grease over them—as a ritual; well, not the bacon grease part.

Note: All the journaling offerings in guide*line* four are meant to be re-read within days of writing them.

Tragic writers like Sylvia Plath, Anais Nin, and Ernest Hemingway used journaling (plus, perhaps, several brown cocktails and pink pills) to bear their trials of life, love, and art. Because of this, I was under the impression journals were specifically for moaning low. Journaling seemed to be a rite of passage for the tortured folk. It appeared journaling was where artists bled out pain. So, I thought I was in right company to scribble my dark nights of the soul onto pages while nursing whiskey in a plastic cup and a half-smoked cigarette. At age 21, if somebody would have shown me a way to make my journal a wonderland of possibility and explained it could be the roadmap to everything I wanted instead of a vacuum of gloom, I would have been on edge to learn how to outline, color, and shine myself up. But, no worry. I figured it out by accident, and you get to be the lucky one who learns how to do all of those colorful things from me.

Journals can hold all your stuff. All your emotions. The high tides and low tides. You won't need to set all your journals on fire. Journals don't have to turn your stomach or remind you how small and insignificant you felt during your last three relationships (I'm talking about me, not you). Journaling is more than a dumping ground for exes and other unhappy endings.

Thirty years and I've got bookshelves of ink-stained journals. I journal WiLD every morning for 25 minutes these days. WiLD is an acronym for **W**riting to **i**magine, **L**isten, and **D**eclare or **D**ecide. Journaling WiLD wrote the maps to many of my dream destinations like losing my first 20 pounds, winning two bodybuilding shows, setting up lives in three major cities without having a job prior to arriving, getting the teaching position I declared, and marrying a man with a beach house (yes, I declared a beach house in my journal and four years later I had one). For six months I journaled and described the Theatre Arts position I wanted. I got it within the year. I was appointed Head of the Theatre Department in a school that didn't have a theatre department before they met me. I declared all these outcomes and more in my journal. I received, in real-life, way above what I expected.

I've got stacks of journals with blank pages awaiting my marks. Now that I publish inspirational journals, my friends and family have to think harder about what to get me for Christmas. I guess I could tell them the name of my favorite pens. Fine point ELITE Uni-Balls.

when I journal something moves, something gets arrested, something shakes, lifts,
becomes unwoven, opens.
sometimes the change will happen in the very moment I'm writing.
sometimes the change is pending, needing me to listen longer, write more, purge more, explore
more, wait. and sometimes the journal helps me notice something has already been changed.

if walls could talk.

They might have been trying to.

Before Egyptians found papyrus, they etched messages onto rock. Archeologists suspect the animal drawings found on cave walls 40,000 years ago delineate hunting conquests. Alongside the pigment-stained bison were other curious markings. What do you think the X's, circles, and squiggly lines on the cave walls symbolized? Maybe they communicated some kind of code. It could have been a kind of diary.

Researchers still wonder.

can I borrow a pen?

For centuries we hankered for dependable instruments for writing. The Chinese carved words into turtle shells with sharp tools. The Romans burned words into wax tablets. The Babylonians carved into clay tablets. The Egyptians used reed pens on papyrus.

We held our breath until, behold... the quill! But you know how bird feathers can be. The tips dry out of ink and break easily. Still, we made-do with our plumes. Then we got the tool that changed record-keeping forever. Okay, that was probably the IBM computer or the iPhone 6, but click back a few centuries. The ballpoint pen was on our desks by 1888. Thank you so much John J. Loud, and also thanks to Laszlo Biro, who later perfected it.

Stacks of tree paper and canisters of ink pens later; artists, writers, business people, and leaders created a lineage of diary keepers. Beethoven kept a diary to record inspiration on nature walks. Comedic writer, Larry David, jotted notes from everyday interactions into his diary to use in sketches for SEINFELD and CURB YOUR ENTHUSIASM. President Ronald Reagan's diary became a best-selling book in 2007, and Oprah Winfrey has been telling her journal five grateful things every day since 1996. I'd like to be a bookmark in Oprah's gratitude journal or any of her journals.

Who isn't intrigued to know what someone with the talent of Beethoven, the comic liquidity of Larry David, the tenacity of Ronald Reagan, and the self-actualized focus of Oprah Winfrey thinks about, worries about, dreams about, and feels every day? I'll speak for my ~~nosy~~ intrigued self.

We covet the private books of our social icons. Anne Frank's diary transformed our lives and ignited an ongoing conversation between nations. John Steinbeck maniacally criticized himself throughout his diary while writing The Grapes of Wrath. Five months of self-denigration led to one of the greatest pieces of literature ever published.

Journals from Anais Nin, Susan Sontag, James Baldwin, and Ernest Hemingway show us how they sourced their genius while also giving us a glimpse at history, framed by their experiences in America and other countries.

Do you own a photo album, baby book, yearbook, or scrapbook—a hardcover version or one stored online? These are modern day time capsules, also diaries. So are the Facebook and Instagram platforms. Like journaling, we post our feelings and opinions on these platforms and they become time capsules *forever* saved in the cloud. They aren't private, though.

Writing for an audience to review, to like, to love, or to leave you a comment is <u>different than</u> <u>journaling WiLD</u>. An audience tends to inspire a performance. Your journal needs to be empty of judgment, ridicule, rightness or wrongness. Your private parts belong in a private place.

when to show your private parts.

I suggest you keep all your journal entries private—initially. Write for yourself, to yourself, with no intention of showing anyone; and you're likely to tell the truth, the whole truth, and nothing but it. Any time you write for public view, you invite an editor. You might censor or write for validation and applause. Public writing usually saddles your Gnome to ride your pen.

The Gnome'll nag you to embellish and make yourself look better or worse, depending on your circumstance or the audience.

who should see what lies beneath?

I won't share any issue from my journal that I haven't examined and resolved. Never—not until I've integrated the message my Interior Voice wants me to hear. The personal details I'm revealing in this book have already been worked through in private. Plus, I'm not fixing to tell you everything about me. A girl should keep some things totally to herself.

After giving *your* Interior Voice ample time to listen, imagine, and speak without becoming diluted with someone else's opinion, and after you've been able to make a decision about your idea or circumstance, then, and only then might you share it with someone.

If you've done all those things and you're still thinking about sharing a journal entry, consider these questions:

▫ **Why do I want to share the entry with *this* person?**

▫ **What am I hoping will happen after sharing this entry with *this* person?**

▫ **Does this entry expose another private issue? Does it reveal something else about me that I'm not ready to share?**

If you are content with the answers, consider a few more things.

Here are some people you might share your journal content with:

A personal coach, therapist, counselor, or mentor for fitness, relationships, business, lifestyle, and spiritual matters

You might also use content from your journal for creative endeavors like in song lyrics, poetry, writings, movies, or visual art. If you do, you will likely need to revise your writing. Revised entries are not the same as writing untamed or journaling WiLD, which you will learn specific details about soon.

However, I do not recommend reading the actual words you've written in your journal to anyone, including your partner, friends, or mom (relative). I repeat, I don't recommend reading verbatim from your journal.

Instead, extract thoughts or realizations from the content.

There is no way you will write untamed if you believe your writing might be put in front of an audience. Writing for a witness other than yourself kills some of your personal wild. Getting unsatisfactory feedback from someone else can kill your wild, too. Journaling untamed is writing without fixing anything before or after you put it on that page. Journaling WiLD is writing raw and unhindered, fully exposing your thoughts. Your entry never needs to be approved by anyone but you.

Keep the unresolved content from your journal, private. If you don't know whether the issue is fully resolved within you, don't share it. Keep your private parts private—between you and your Interior Voice.

If you desperately need an audience to listen to your journal entries, assemble your dog and cat, a neighbor's bird, and your Aunt Bertha's fish. Give them a reading when your aunt leaves for the grocery store.

Your journal documents your secrets, motivations, expulsions, triumphs, and fears. For the style of journaling I'm presenting in this book, keep the entries privy to your eyes only until you've worked through the content and derived insights and revelations.

But listen, your life *could* curve the pitch. Unforeseen changes could happen. For example, you could become the President of the PTA, a talk show host with a bigger audience than Ellen, an iconic blues drummer, a world-renowned crayon artist, or a celebrated International trapeze flyer. If any of these appointments should happen, well... once you pass into that next realm—uh hum—you know... die, someone is probably gonna find your private journals.

Pause. Pause again for suspense.

We *are* gonna read em. Sorry—I really am sorry, but *we are definitely* going to read those private journals of yours!

And seriously, if you happened upon your great great grandmother's red, satin diary in your mother's attic, wouldn't you read it?

We each know on some level, one's private journal may be the only written record where thoughts rest, uncensored.

colors.

Some people drink cocktails to mellow out. Some go running. My mom shopped. Whenever she said *I need to run into Kmart to grab something*, my brother and I heard *I'll find you two in a few hours*. We'd split up. My little brother parked his body near the GIJoe toys and the footballs. I headed for the life-sized dolls and the books. There was no danger in my eight-year-old brother and ten-year-old me playing unsupervised in Kmart. We lived in Iowa.

Not far from picture and chapter books were the art supplies.
What?! 120 crayons and markers?
I didn't even own the 64-box of crayons with the built-in sharpener, yet. I tried to score it at Christmas, but I got a 24-box instead. Everybody had those. Tammi had a 64-box, and Laura had one, too (those were my 1st and 2nd grade friends, names not changed).

Why did I want all those crayons? Options. I wanted to color without limits. I wanted to experiment outside the primary colors and into the stratosphere. I wanted choices.

I have never, ever owned a magical crayola set of 120's or 64's. I did, however, own 64 total crayons, if I counted all my nubby, de-papered ones. My broken stash didn't boast names like Sienna or Periwinkle. I was quite aware I was using basic Purple and Brown even when the wrappers peeled off. Still, I produced gobs of art with all my crayons.

That's what artists do. They create from whatever they're given. I'm an artist. I don't use crayons much now. I use dumbbells and yoga poses. I paint and make clay jewelry. I wrote song lyrics for years. Now, I write poetry. I created a Theatre Arts program for at-risk teens. I created a youth yoga program for The City University of New York. I am a creator. And despite your resume, you are too.

Whether you dawn a feather boa and torch the cabaret stage or wiggle your nose to make another Great Lake appear off the coast of Michigan or julienne carrots for a stir-fry; you are a creator. You are the artist of your Self, coloring your life with the tools in your box. Your tools happen to be your beliefs, your visions, and your decisions. You don't need 120 colors to create the life you want. You just need clarity. Vision. Confidence.

What does this have to do with journaling? EVERYTHING.

Journaling will show you how you've used the tools in your color box to create the life you have. Journaling will also reveal your options. It will give you choices. **Journaling will become the tool you can use to carve, color, and create a life that fulfills you.**

between the lines

guide*line* two : tell the truth.

my entries show what I allow and what I repel from my life.

Your journal will expose your Interior Voice, a Voice beyond your vocalized voice.
The Interior Voice speaks for your whole Self.

Do you remember a time when you gave exceptional advice to someone and thought, *Gee, I wish I'd written that down?* You are wiser than you've believed. If you were to divulge thoughts and insights in a conversation, you'd fail to capture every pearl of wisdom dropped from your lips. Some of the words from your vocalized voice get saved by the person listening to you, but most of them vaporize into the air. When you write in your journal, your whole Self speaks. You can parse out your thoughts and capture them on the page. You can return to them, add to them, and understand yourself from them. Your wisdom gets recorded, known, then integrated.

Your Interior Voice has so much to tell you.

Messages from your Interior Voice can come by noticing how you feel. That's easy to do. Certainly you're aware that you feel more energized when you wear the red cape and invisible in the taupe raincoat. You prefer thin-crust over deep-pan because your stomach doesn't bloat after you eat it. Generally, you know what makes you feel good, and you'd rather feel that way.

Pay attention to your thoughts and you'll hear your Interior Voice. I'm sure you have a grasp on some of your thoughts. You think it's of value to wait for the cars to stop before you cross the street. You think you oughta chew the steak before you swallow it. You think it makes sense to put your clothes on right-side out (or is it right-side in?).

But what if your thoughts tell you you're too old to start your dream doggie bakery business? What if they tell you you'll never get rid of the extra 25 pounds on your mid-section no matter what you try? What's happening to make you think you're destined to remain single for an eternity? Why do you feel you're not smart enough to apply for the scholarship? If you *regularly and often* have thoughts and feelings that keep you from the joy and fulfillment you want, you need to challenge those thinking disasters.

Your thoughts influence the way you feel, and feelings live in your body. Together your thoughts and feelings drive the choices you make. This could be problematic if you are choosing to go against yourself. Your journal will give you eyes to see, ears to hear, and awareness to feel whether this is happening to you.

Your thoughts are like mental race cars. With upwards of 60,000 thoughts racing around your head every day and night, you could easily get jammed up by thinking disasters making you believe you're out of the running for the things you want. If you really desire to have, feel, and do the things you've placed in your dream bubbles, you'll need to make an effort to figure out which thoughts are jamming you so you can redirect that traffic.

Let's return to your feelings, the more pervasive ones. They are easier to access. If you *regularly feel* worried, mortified, exhausted, pissed, dreary, apathetic, or pathetic in any part of your life, regardless of your library of self-help books and high-ticket "I'm okay" workshops, you might take pause and ask: What am I regularly thinking about to feel this way? Examine the thoughts that anchor you to that trash.

Equally beneficial, figure out what made you feel so devoted, steady, exuberant, fascinated, enlivened, focused, loyal, and daring that time you outdid yourself to claim victory. What were you thinking when you leaped into the goal that brought so much fulfillment that your cheeks ached from smiling? Do you want to leap to victory again? Of course. Do you remember what you believed when you were magical? How could you remember? Your thoughts are speeding Corvettes. 60,000 red ones. On a daily course. That's worse than Atlanta traffic. You can slow them down, though. You can park them and take a closer look.
Get your journal.

hands are for... declaring

◎ **Make a list of 40 things you want to do, be, have, or experience in the next 20 years.**

drive the Corvette.

It takes a wild amount of fortitude to have what you want. This is especially true if you desire to lose 10, 20, or 50 pounds. Weight-loss becomes a "must" before your wedding, a priority before your cruise to Aruba, and garners all your attention before your high school reunion. That's why you hire a hot trainer and lunge till you can barely walk. You eat plants until you pee green and drink enough water to challenge a camel. You're willing to hijack your comforts and go pedal to the metal on discipline, because you really want your dress to zip up.

Swoosh. You lose 17 lbs. Once your target is hit, your foot loses pressure. You return to doing what you used to do: treadmill walks while texting, healthy meals at the beginning of the week (if you remember), a Snickers to hold you over, and cereal before bed. Your personal trainer stash gets redistributed between Venti Frappuccinos and Zappos. You return to "your reality"; a good sport, yet gloomy. Definitely disappointed. You're back at your default setting.

Why? You changed your actions, but forgot to change your mind. Your one true obstacle is and has always been—your mind. It's a beautiful mind. Wildly creative and powerful. This is good if you understand how to power it toward getting what you want. Your mind is creating your life experience.

You can create the body you imagine—by journaling. You can. You can connect with an amazing life partner by journaling. It's true. You can. You can save money to buy that home on a mountain in the Poconos by journaling. You can start that doggie business. What do you want?

There are some areas in your life where you simply thrive, and it doesn't feel difficult to maintain that success either, right? Think of them now. However, everyone has an area in life that could use a little more shine. We generally have five compartments where we live, *5 parts of being*. They include *Finances, Health, Spirituality, Relationships, and Career*. One or two of these parts has traffic that needs to move in a different direction in order to bring you fulfillment.

Which comes to mind for you?

I'll go first...

Love relationships. You knew I was going to say that. I conquered my body issues during my 20's and 30's, organized my finances in my 30's, and confronted my spiritual stuff in my 40's. But I have yet to rest fulfilled around partner/relationship stuff. I've begun to re-write my beliefs about love and partnering, because, by golly, I'd like to **stay** with one dude one day. Please nod if you can relate, so I'm not hangin' out here by myself.

I already told you about my friendship-ever-after relationships. Exes don't hate me (it's been mutual), and they still trust me (not totally mutual). I think it's sweet and all, but I'm still single. I'm willing to challenge my beliefs about relationships, because I've decided to make myself available to someone this time. I journal about this. It's okay to want what you want. It's okay to avail yourself to be fulfilled by something you've never wanted before, never experienced before, or something you have failed at before.

hands are for... deciding

○ Are you available for fulfillment? In which area(s) of your life?

Before you answer, consider your *5 parts of being*:

Finances = savings, bills, spending, investments

Health = body image, eating habits, movement habits, relaxation, self-care, inner talk

Spirituality = charity/donation of time and money, conservation of natural resources, meditation or inward gaze (reflection), devotion to a Source of Spiritual power, reverence to nature and the environment

Relationship = partnership, friends, networking, parents and relatives, animals

Career = job placement, role, income, value and contribution, education, hobbies

○ **Pick one or two *parts of being* that you want to explore.**
○ **List or describe what you'd like to experience.**

You can get ideas from your list of the 40 things you want to have, be, do, or experience.

○ **Why do you believe it's been challenging to find fulfillment in this *part of being*?**

Your Interior Voice knows why.
This question may require several journal entries.

Continue to explore these desires with your journal.

i've been thinking 'bout it...

When my fitness clients want to lose weight and elevate their health I ask *what are you doing now to move toward your goal?* I often get answers like *I exercise once a week* or *I just joined the gym* or *I don't eat carbs anymore*. These are promising answers. They are starting points. I dig deeper.

What did you do to lose weight in the past? How did you gain it back? What is happening in your life that deters you from creating your ideal body?

I ask them to describe their goals.

How will you look when you reach your goal? How will you feel about yourself when you reach your goal? How will your life change when you reach your goal?

To drop 25 pounds, improve posture, lower blood sugars, and increase stamina, a client's self-definition must change before they'll see physical changes. The biggest leap they need to make is away from doubt and fear. They must rehearse what could be possible until they believe it.

Your beliefs are the source of your power. Read that again. I'll probably say it eight more times in this book. Your beliefs are your power. I reached for my pen when I first learned this.

When I decided to enter a bodybuilding show, I had to upgrade my self-definition and change what I believed was possible. Throughout my teens and twenties I was plagued by an eating disorder. My disorder had no scientific name that I knew of. I ate like a linebacker, so however you'd classify that—I had that disorder. Even though I wasn't an athlete in high school, and even though I had never seen muscle definition on my body before, I decided I was gonna get bodybuilding ready. For nine months I trained and imagined the outcomes I wanted using my journal. Writing new visions dismantled my fears. I checked in with my journal every day until the contest. I won two first place trophies during the summer of 2000.

When I decided to move from L.A. to New York City, I had to construct beliefs about how I would do it seeing as though I only had $400 under my futon. After four months of morning pages in my L.A. kitchen and after visualizing a life in NYC, I changed what I believed—then I moved. I got full-time employment at a premier gym in mid-town four days after arriving in New York. I became the top female personal trainer in that gym within two and a half years. I believed these things were going to happen to me before they did. I met, in real-life, the Self and life I wrote about and visualized in my journal. I achieved seemingly impossible dreams over and over again.

Choices. Options. Decisions. You can choose how your mind will move your feet. This is the great gift of journaling. Are you gonna press the mental pedal and drive toward a life that fulfills you or parade with the backed up traffic toward Mundane Junction?

floor it.

Who on the planet wouldn't want to ramp up their financial profile, find or improve a relationship, drop two dress sizes, or finish a heartfelt project? You want to get out of debt. You want to feel confident on a date. You want to stop procrastinating. These are amazing aspirations. When I've asked my fitness students: *Are you journaling about the life you want?*

Some return these responses:

- *Ah...that's a good idea. Journaling.*

- *Yes, Michelle. I know about journaling. I used to journal in high school, college...*

- *No, I haven't started journaling yet.*

- *I am thinking hard about how I can make these changes.*

They slip journaling into the glove box and parade toward the Junction. Maybe journaling would make them more confident. Maybe it could help them become conscious of their meals. Maybe it would make them aware of how they react in relationships, keep them focused on finishing their projects, increase the dough in their wallets. But, I know what else they're thinking. Journaling reminds them of something they had to do in touchy-feely classes from school when introspection was an elective, not a personal choice. The only grown-ups who have petty time to soul-search and cry in a journal are Anais Nin groupies.

I get it, and I understand. Being a grown-up *is* serious business. Adults need to be practical and make goals come by mature means. A $10,000 weekend of fist-pumping and affirmation screaming—that's definitely a grown-up way to get to a goal.

Grown-ups would rather call their therapists and tell them what they told them last week, the same story they told the week before; the same story they've told their best friend three times, the same story they told the air that day they searched two floors of the parking garage for the car.

I get it. Journaling takes time—10-25 minutes. And dedication. To their hearts. Grown-ups have other obligations, jobs, and parental duties that carry more necessity than dedication to the heart. Wizzing the mini-van to the football field to grab the boys and ten of his friends, then rushing home to turn the crock pot to warm—this takes precedence over journaling for 25 minutes in the morning before the house needs pancakes. How could a grown-up find time to journal before bed? They're way too tired. They only have enough energy to scroll Instagram for exercise videos, then do the same on Facebook, then check google news, then see if anyone LIKED their likes.

Who has the time to examine feelings or pay attention to fulfillment? Not grown-ups. They're too serious for such shenanigans. They'd prefer to "think" about change.

Thinking about changing isn't altogether worthless. Thinking *alone* could surely guarantee one outcome—the awareness that you will endlessly nurse agita with no way to relieve it. Eye-closing and hand-holding resolved the situation for Thelma and Louise. You need to choose something with more traction.

If you're a grown-up or close to being one, and if confidence, freedom, or fulfillment are of any interest to you, let me give you some perspective.

Thinking your way into desirable outcomes is similar to expecting a hoarder to bring you a penny from their humble home. Granted, the hoarder is somewhat familiar with the clutter. They live in it every day. But, if they locate a penny in there, they'd be lucky. A hoarder collects stuff over the length of their life. Depending on how long that is and depending on how much space their clutter covers, it could take forever to find a coin. The hoarder would probably give up looking due to exhaustion or cave into overwhelm.

A small task can pose a big problem if the task involves navigating a cluttered environment.

But there is a way to find that penny. Let's say this house is yours. It isn't, but for the sake of making this point, it's your junk house for the next two minutes (months). Remember, you also drive a Corvette. Life ain't awful.

You set aside one day a week to sort each room. Start small, like in the hallway. It won't tax as much energy as the bathroom or garage. Throw away the mound of single socks by the stairs. You'll never find their matches. The skirts and pants hanging on the banister can go in a box. Put it in the bedroom when it's filled. Okay, fill two boxes, but no more than that. Check the sizes. If the item doesn't fit anymore, label a separate box: Salvation Army. Don't keep everything. You can hang the items you're keeping in the closet after you clean the bedroom next week.

Take two days to clean the kitchen. Empty the fridge and wipe the shelves clean. The fridge will give you the most satisfaction, because you can toss out most of the food. It's spoiled.

If you're focusing on losing weight, keep the healthy food. Use the same process to organize the cabinets. Trash the expired food and chipped dishes, wipe the shelves, then re-shelf with the desirable food and dishes.

Make your way through your entire house like this. It might take a few months to purge and organize the stuff you're keeping, maybe longer, but you can do it if you remain steady. And it's worth it. Think of the benefits. Your couch won't make weird crunching sounds when you sit. Your slacks won't be wrinkled anymore. The bathroom floor will lose that stick that grabs your slippers in the middle of the night. And you'll finally find your passport.

Set up a routine to clean your house once a week or for 25 minutes every day. After you've hung your clothes in closets, vacuumed your floors, and cleared the dresser of spare change, you can bring me a mason jar full of found pennies.

(By the end of this book, you'll have a clean house, pennies, and a Corvette floored toward the stars.)

Your mind is like this house. It's cluttered with memories, thought patterns, and beliefs you've been forming and validating since you got here.

Your cluttered mind will benefit from regular housekeeping.

Journaling regularly declutters your mind so you can locate what you've been looking for.

Your thinking mind is a cluttered thruway of speeding Corvettes, racing in the same direction day after day, unless you construct another thruway that takes you where you want to go.

hands are for... de-cluttering

◎ **What have you considered releasing or letting go of? Why?**

◎ **How will this release de-clutter your life?**

◎ **What in your life have you considered starting or adding?**

For both questions consider ➡ jobs, obligations, activities, roles, and reactions.

You can also consider anything you've journaled concerning your *5 parts of being*.

No problem can be solved from the same level of consciousness that created it.

ALBERT EINSTEIN

backseat drivers.

Out of the 60,000 thoughts you will think today, your subconscious mind is responsible for 85% of them. Your subconscious mind is your memory portal. It stores the data from your life experience so far. Your perceptions and the conclusions you make about yourself and your life are informed by your subconscious mind.

Your subconscious mind is in your driver's seat.

If losing weight and keeping it off has been nearly impossible or if staying out of debt is an uphill challenge, you've got a reservoir of subconscious data keeping you attached to these difficulties. I call the subconscious mind the PROGRAM, because it has so much influence over how you feel and what you do. It informs what you believe is possible.

What's in your PROGRAM? What are you thinking? What do you believe? Remember, you can tell what you're thinking and believing by noticing how you feel.

Your beliefs and feelings run on autopilot, because, well—your PROGRAM runs on autopilot. That means you must consciously explore your thoughts, feelings and beliefs if you want to redirect them.

Consciousness. You activate your conscious mind when you PAY ATTENTION to what's happening in the present moment. The PRINCIPLE mind, or conscious thinking, is utilized 5-10% of the time each day.

Imagine carpooling to work with your co-worker, Jenny, while listening to the book, *E is for Evidence* on the Audible app. You're both mesmerized by Sue Grafton's mystery. Jenny asks if you'll pause the audiobook and explain the part she didn't understand. You make a sharp right and pull into the parking space closest to the door to your office. That parking space is usually free because you and Jenny always arrive early. You park the car while retelling, in detail, the part Jenny missed.

Who was driving your car while you were listening to the book? You were. Who parked the car while you retold the details to Jenny? You did, of course. Your subconscious mind did it. Your PROGRAM drove and parked. Your PROGRAM has been driving the same way to work five days a week for the last 16 years. The route, the stops, the turns, all the places where traffic slows, and the perfect parking spot has been memorized by your PROGRAM. Your PRINCIPLE mind listened to the story. You didn't have to pay full conscious attention to driving. Your PROGRAM could retrieve the mental imprint of driving on autopilot because it was rehearsed so often. Your PRINCIPLE mind was delegated to solving Grafton's mystery.

The third segment of your mind, according to Carl Jung, is superconsciousness. Jungian theory suggests there is a portal of Infinite Potentials that you can access through superconscious thinking. You can select an outcome from Infinite Potentials based on the thoughts, beliefs, and pictures you decide to let marinate *regularly and often* in your imagination.

You can choose to believe in and visualize the kind of outcome you desire, even if you've never experienced it before. Your chosen outcome can seem illogical. It can seem foreign to your history. You have the option to imagine what you truly want when you employ the superconscious mind or, as I call it, POSSIBILITY mind.

POSSIBILITY mind gets utilized less than 5% of the time. Journaling WiLD utilizes POSSIBILITY mind much more than that. With POSSIBILITY thinking you can choose an outcome even if it's **not** supported by the evidence in your PROGRAM. This is big!

POSSIBILITY thinking doesn't need evidence from your life experience. If the outcome you desire is POSSIBLE, and if you maintain an unwavering belief that it can happen, persistent POSSIBILITY thinking makes it likely that it will.

POSSIBILITY journaling is one of the offerings you get to practice in guide*line* four.

understand your mind.
some of the data you've stored in it will keep you safe.
some will keep you caged.
you don't have to believe everything you've stored in your head.

hands are for... listening

Do you remember playing pretend as a kid (age 6-11)?

◎ **What childhood scenarios did you make-believe? What pretend role(s) did you play? Describe them in detail.**

Now, recall two of your childhood friends. Describe each of them below.

You can consider how they looked, their favorite games or activities, their relationships with their siblings, the things they talked about, the way they spoke, their personal environment like their bedroom or house or their favorite places to play.

◎ **Name of friend #1_____ . Description.**

◎ **Name of friend #2_____ . Description.**

Review the descriptions of your friends.

◎ **How are they similar to you now?**
◎ **How are they different from you now?**

I'm in love with my imagination,

a love

I rekindled.

after hustling to secure a bank account balance greater than $20, then a mortgage,

then mutual funds,

it became ever-so-challenging to stay faithful to

my imagination.

I wanted to befriend it the way I did when my bedroom was in the basement.

I was 13.

I would lie in a bed surrounded by wallpaper flowers.

my turntable blasted Prince up through the floor boards while my mind played future pictures,

real-feeling scenes far away from how my life looked.

daydreaming, a child's version of planning,

took me everywhere

for free—

gave me a preview of what was

coming.

imagining.

it's not an enemy of time-management, it's not a way of procrastinating.

it's magical,

same as it was

when my bedroom had wallpaper flowers.

the mirror.

When I tell my exercise students to observe their bodies in the mirror during the workout, I get various responses.

Yuck. Really? I don't like it. I look terrible. I can't. Okay, okay!
I also get the sneaky, non-compliant response. She says *okay, okay*, but doesn't look. Ever. She looks down. Looks at her feet. She looks at me. Not sneaky enough, because I know what's up. She doesn't feel comfortable.

I insist my clients use a mirror to help maintain proper posture. Many of us have no idea whether we're aligned or lopsided. Over time, misalignments start to feel normal. Anything that feels normal becomes habituated. Becoming aware, or paying attention, is how to address the unconscious, auto-piloted habits. I maintain that clients use the mirror to keep their shoulders relaxed, instead of shrugged to the ears. I ask them to make sure their chest is open, not concave. Their neck needs to be long, not stuck in a turtle shell. An aligned spine supports maximum performance and reduces injury.

My clients want these things, so why resist looking into a mirror?
The mirror confronts. It reveals what one might have avoided looking at. It's common to go through life without seeing ourselves, without reflecting on who we are.

reflection.

When I was a performer, our rehearsal rooms had floor to ceiling mirrors. Examining ourselves was part of our training. We observed ourselves on film, in photos, in the mirror, and in vocal recordings.

Usually the first time people observe themselves on film or hear themselves recorded they're horrified.

□ Is that what I sound like in real life?

□ Do I walk like that?

□ Look at my body. Is my _____ that big, small, wide, loose, skinny, awful?

□ It's terrible. (I'm not good enough).

If we hold any secret belief of not-enoughness, looking at our reflection in a mirror or hearing a recording of our voice can flick a switch that blasts the volume on this belief, sending us into flight, fright, or freezing. I've witnessed clients cover their eyes, plug their ears, look away, leave the room, or stay but heckle their reflection. They'd rather protect themselves from the barrage of insults from their Gnome.

• *This is exactly why you don't get the attention your sister does. You're homely and strange. Just look at you!*

• *See. Told ya! That's why you don't have a man. Your boobs are non-existent and your butt looks like you've spent half your life sitting.*

- *Who do you think you are? You're a wanna-be impersonating someone who's educated and properly trained. Stop trying to sound like somebody you're not and never will be.*
- *Oh girl. Why don't you give up on those legs and gut? Or find a football team that'll recruit you for tackling.*

Remember the salty fella in my thoughts, my nasty Gnome? When I first heard a recording of my voice, I panicked that I might sound like an eight-year-old all my life. In college when the fat on my legs went viral, encasing my belly and butt, cameras and mirrors became kryptonite. I'd stand behind people in photos. I avoided full-length mirrors unless I was fully dressed. If I accidentally saw my bare body in a full mirror, I'd launch an attack. Except it wasn't totally me voicing the attack.

My orange-eyed, thick-knuckled Gnome would snicker:
- *Michelle, what's wrong with you? You look like a scared baby with your shoulders hunched up to your ears.*
- *Put some clothes on. What are you thinking, walking around showing your fat knees and gross thighs to the world? It ain't cute. Better wear those full skirts. Hide that fat. Do it NOW before anyone else sees you.*
- *Yeah, great smile except for those small, gapped teeth. Keep your mouth closed, girl. Grin.*
- *You're not as cute as you were as a kid. You must be going through the ugly stage. Too bad it's lasting such a long time.*
- *You're just fat. That's all there is to it. Fat! And you eat too much to do anything about it. Pathetic.*

That was hard to write. I remember hearing all that stuff and journaling about it when I sought to change my body.

Here's what else you need to know. During those same Gnome-stalking-my-body years, my magical interior Child Self danced with an amazing social life. I sang to sold out crowds. I had 500 friends. Folks asked me why I smiled so much (and yes, that was before I had braces). You see, one aspect of my life was warm peach pie. The area that pained me, my body and health, was a burnt meatloaf. I refused to look at the meatloaf. The full-length mirror magnified pain that I refused to fully confront.

I wasn't a total vampire. I rehearsed for performances in front of mirrors. I pretended to sing into a camera using a mirror. But that's as far as I looked... until the day I learned to use the mirror to create what I wanted.

Rewind back to Chicago at 23 years old—single, stuffing chocolate chip cookie dough down my throat before bed, legal pads as journals, tears, Sade records, riding a ferris wheel around WTF every day. You remember. (I'm feeling like Quentin Tarantino using all these flashbacks).

My vapid job and expanding thighs left me despondent. I wished for a fairy godmother to turn my bus pass into a plane ticket to anywhere but my life. I journaled on weekends. After six months of journaling the same sad tale, the journal and I decided to give notice—to the job and the sadness. We (my journal and I) had no idea what we'd do after we quit, but we agreed it had to include using my Voice.

It was the second time I sat in Harvey's office. The first was the interview that got me hired two months after moving to Chicago. I scooched to the edge of my seat. Two words came out, words Harvey did not want to hear. *I quit.* Right after I said them, I received the first of several gifts that would follow. Harvey asked me to reconsider (*no*); said he'd be challenged to find a replacement for me (okay... a compliment, but still *no*), then requested I stay for five weeks instead of two to help train the replacement (deal). First gift—three extra weeks of income my journal and I hadn't allocated. Score.

I got the call one week later—the second gift. I'd previously sent a demo to a production house overseas. Out of the blue, they offered me a two-month singing gig in Osaka, Japan. Insert celebratory chimes and confetti-sized stardust—plus add back some *happy*. Gift number three—a month off work before starting rehearsals for the Japan gig. No more crying. I journaled in hip cafes, positioned new dreams into bubbles, wrote song lyrics, and recorded demos. I stopped buying cookie dough.

Okay, hold up. I'm getting to the mirror part, but these prior gifts need to be mentioned. Each of them was influenced by decisions I'd written about and imagined in my journal.

Elliot was one of five male dancers cast to perform in Osaka. The other two girls casted were lean gymnasts. I was hired to sing lead—tight body not necessary. The costume designers dressed me in shorts over thick, lace tights so my legs wouldn't look fat onstage. The other girls' shorts showed their flesh. I was used to hiding.

At the hotel pool, Elliot commented:

You have a nice shape, Michelle. What are you gonna do about your weight?

He didn't laugh or smile. Bold question.

Uh...

Was he actually asking me this?

I don't know, Elliot. I've tried everything.

I laughed.

Elliot didn't.

He told me about his weight struggles. Clearly he'd mastered them. Elliot had sculpted muscles and advanced jumping and dancing skills. He taught aerobic classes in Florida.

In addition to the six days of shows we were contracted to perform, Elliot worked out in the hotel gym every day.

You are beautiful, Michelle. You're always gonna be cast as the ingenue, the lead... till you gain too much weight.

Hmmm?

I used to be way overweight, Michelle. I understand how you feel. But I got committed and changed my body. What are you gonna do?

I tried committing too, Elliot. I'd been trying to "commit" since I was 16 years old. My journal knew.

Imagine how you'd look if you lost that weight, girl... Just go for it. You'd be so beautiful. You are now, but imagine how much more beautiful. Do you realize how far you could go?

That did it for me. I hadn't imagined how far I could go. I'd stopped thinking about my body, period. Or that's what I'd tried to do. In actuality, I thought about my body so much, it was distressing.

Elliot said I was beautiful. I had resigned in consensus with my Gnome that I was just okay-looking, not all-that, mostly fat with gapped teeth, and probably oughta keep growing my hair long to keep everyone from noticing my physical flaws.

A part of me wanted to believe Elliot. I wrote to my journal about it every morning in Japan when I went down for breakfast. Soft scrambled eggs, one piece of toast, pickles, and coffee with goat's milk. *How would I look? How would I feel?* I described it in my journal.

I must interject; beauty and being slim are not synonymous. The real issue for me was that at 23 years-old, I ate enough to feed a rugby team. God knows, I would have so many health issues right now if I didn't take control of my eating habits back then. Also, I harbored a low opinion of myself. I ate to soothe the not good-enoughness, the odd attraction to older men, the block around celebrating my accomplishments—all my hogwash. I carried more than just excess body-fat. I lived in a body suit that expressed my baggage of lies more than it expressed the real me.

Back to the gifts. Servings of food in Japan were a quarter the size of Chicago servings, plus we performed six days a week. I lost the first five pounds effortlessly—gift number four. When I returned to Chicago, I took inspiration from the visions I wrote in my journal and started taking classes with Anna. Anna was a hefty aerobic instructor with a distinct accent. Polish or

Russian or Spanish. She spoke all three languages. Anna had lost 100 pounds and taught her classes like she was aggressively aiming to lose thirty more. She was tough. I stood near her during class, even though I had to leave after fifteen minutes because I couldn't breathe. Within a few months, I hung next to Anna for the full hour.

Alas, the mirror and gift number five! After class with Anna, I'd stand close to the studio mirrors. Turning to the side, I'd imagine my arms sculpted. Turning to the back, I'd pretend the cellulite was gone from my legs. I'd see a flat belly and a small waist. I didn't see what was actually in the mirror, I saw my body the way I wanted to see it. I imagined it. I did this every week. I wrote my workouts in my journal every week. I described how I'd act and what I'd do when I lost the weight in my journal. I wrote the future vision of my body like it had already happened in real life.

A year later while shopping for toothpaste, I looked up at the sound of my name.
Michelle? Wow. Is that you?
I recognized the guy from the gym.
You look great.
I was wearing ripped jeans and an orange tank. Jeans never fit my thighs when I was 20 pounds heavier.
You lost so much weight! You look like a totally different person.
I was.

I overcame my resistance to looking in a mirror. I used my reflection and my Voice to conquer what had been a slippery goal. Your journal is your mirror. Look into it. See yourself. You will never change anything you're not willing to look at. Witness your feelings. Ask questions. Listen for answers. Your journal, your mirror, has something to tell you. Listen. Journal to imagine, listen, and declare the life experience you truly want.

By the way, my Gnome never quieted his opinions about me. He shared my bus seat the day I told Harvey I didn't want to work at the radio station anymore. He met me at breakfast while I journaled in Japan. He laughed at me when I couldn't breathe in Anna's classes. He tapped his knuckly toes while I imagined my new body in the mirror. That little critter was shaking his head at me just a few minutes ago.

I'm not buddy-buddy with my troll-Gnome, but I've figured out how to handle his two-penny advice. Your Gnome will pop into your reflection now and again. Dudes like that never totally disappear, so get used to them. Let him spit to satisfy his little "need" to play a role in your psyche. Then hush him away.

(Gnomes fit easily into the back pockets of your jeans. Sit often.)

I'll give you the lowdown on ways to handle your Gnome during guide*line* four. For now, give the little dude a side smile when he **butts** into your life, and keep on declaring what you want.

hands are for... listening

◎ **Is there an area in your life where you keep experiencing the same types of <u>unwanted</u> outcomes?**

For example, are you experiencing similar problems at your job no matter where you work?
Do you endure the same unwanted issues no matter who you date?
Do you procrastinate even if you start early or make a schedule?
Is there an area of your life that feels like a house of mirrors?

◎ **Write your thoughts about any area where this is true.**

Circumstance does not make the man,
it reveals him to himself.

JAMES ALLEN, from As a Man Thinketh

ink-stained

untame yourself.

spend time in the wild.

your journal can get you there.

untangle the vines from your lips,

cords that suffocate

sound

and understanding.

uncoil the restraints from your fingers

that threaten stillness.

you need them to move.

upset the stillness,

rattle the quiet.

let wild injure the familiar.

it won't hurt.

it will heal.

rush bravery down your arm,

unleash your Voice through your pen.

claim the page.

this is a call to journal.

guide*line* three : set your shy pen free.

your fears are feeding your resistance.
what if you could plow through resistance?
what if you dropped every facade and purely became your Self?

untame yourself.

I am untidy and unabashedly blemished in my journal. I write with raw expression, WiLD and free. I do not uphold rules about grammar or content. I say what I wish, the way I wish to say it. This style of journaling unbinds my Interior Voice so it can come through purely and vulnerably, wise and revealing.

Every morning I journal WiLD.
WiLD is:

W   **Writing**/journaling
i   Using your **imagination** to visualize
L   **Listening** and paying attention to your Interior Voice
D   **Declaring**/Deciding

You used to be raw. Remember? You were wild before you got tamed, no different than the rest of us. We all get programmed by our environments; educated into society's standards. We learn the ropes of adulthood from the decided authorities: the media, statistics, Ms. Johnson, your eighth grade Humanities teacher, your mama, the popular girl who drove the convertible BMW in 11th grade, the Kardashian with the big... uh, paycheck, and Oprah, of course. Clearly, some of the sources that tamed us could be strained through better discretion, as also could some of the thoughts and beliefs that we've let tame us.

Your mind was massively porous from the time you were a toddler through grade school. During those formative years you went through a refinement process. Kicking and wailing got replaced by learning to use the magic word to get what you wanted—*please*. And even though it took 45 failed attempts, you were taught to take turns when interacting with others. However, you were also taught what to think to be "practical", what to do to be "logical", and who you needed to become to be "acceptable".

You were once wild and ferociously curious. Even if you can't remember sticking everything in your mouth to taste for meaning, you did investigative stuff like that. Before you were tamed, you were decisive about what you didn't like without needing anyone else to validate your choices. Recall pursing your lips to block the second spoonful of those over-cooked peas. Recall the scream and slobber-fest that got you out of that crib and into a warm lap. You were but a foot long, yet unapologetically game about doing what you needed to do to get to a better feeling state.

Sure, you were simpler at 15 months old. At 9 years old, too. You hadn't become as mysterious as you are now. You hadn't been exposed to reputation, obligation, or limitation, yet. You hadn't learned that some of the stuff you wanted would be out of your reach, or that the family you were born into limited your options; that some folks got privileges, others didn't. You hadn't learned that age, looks, and proper education would determine what you could do, be, or have.

Becoming tamed happens slowly. There's no one to blame, really. The big folks, baby-sitters, and teachers in charge did what was needed to get you ready for society. They weaned you off dangerous sports like eating the electrical socket with a metal fork and completing the Sharpie Picasso you started scribbling into Grandma's table cloth. Most taming was necessary.

Conclusions you've drawn about life have also tamed you. Some of those conclusions have steered you away from your natural inclinations. When you were raw and pure, you might have loved talking about your curiosities, till you learned you oughta *shut up, because you're nothing but annoying.* So now, you don't posit questions, even when you don't understand or don't agree with something. You might have been tamed to follow your family's push to pursue a medical profession, though you've been a natural dancer since the day you first heard music. Your armoire might hold all your bow ties and starched suits, though as a young boy you longed to paint your nails yellow and wear purple tights. You might have the most beautiful smile, but you were warned that girls who smile too much aren't taken seriously.

Or like me, you might have seen your bachelor father taste from a buffet of lady-friends barely eight years older than you. No wonder I got tamed into thinking men twenty years my senior were attractive. Or like me, maybe you were raised never to boast. *Stay humble or you'll fall and embarrass yourself.* So, like me, you're tamed to reject compliments. Or maybe you continually enroll in classes for certifications because you're tamed to believe you're **still** not adequately prepared to step into your goals. I was tamed to feel that way. And also, like I did, you might hide your body *because it's fat and overly sexualized.* I was tamed to believe people would either joke about my chubbiness or men would think I was easy if I wore revealing clothes.

I have journaled WiLD to overcome these unsupportive PROGRAMS. You can, too.

By the way, if you ever wanna boast, it's okay in my company. I'd love to hear your good news. I'm all ears for your bravery and fortitude. I have certainly stopped hanging my head low just so others won't get offended by my triumphs. I've decided to feel good whenever I choose, the way I choose. You are free to do the same. Can I get an Amen?!

hands are for... reflecting

◎ **How have you been tamed?**
◎ **In what ways have you embraced your wild?**

You are intuitive. If a snapshot of a psychic with long, black nails hovering over a crystal ball flashed in your mind, I'm not talking about that. If you don't know you're naturally intuitive, it's only because you haven't followed your hunches often enough or trusted your gut when the feeling told you what to do. If you have not acknowledged the whispering under your skin, you will. Soon, you will. You will meet your Interior Voice. You will meet your WiLD.

Journaling WiLD is a 10-25 minute, free-style writing exercise that reveals messages, information, and guidance from your Interior Voice.

There is a witness within you, with eyes and ears that have seen and heard you up till now. There is a Wise-sage, a Child, an Angel, and a Gnome Self within you. They are all a part of you, each with a Voice and a story about where you've been and where you need to go to be protected and fulfilled. They are aspects of your Interior Voice, aspects of your psyche. When you let them speak, you'll learn more about yourself than anyone outside could tell you.

hands are for... listening

You are fueling your life experience with the words you profess most often about yourself.

Listen to yourself.

The "L" from WiLD is *Listen*.

Throughout the day, pay attention to the words you choose to describe your abilities, feelings, and expectations.

For the next two days:

◎ **Listen to your inner talk/inner chatter.**
How do you speak to/about yourself? What do you say? Do you duck away from compliments? How do you speak about other people? Do you gossip or praise?
Do you talk over people instead of listening and sharing the conversation? Do you embellish your abilities to heighten your self-concept? Do you acknowledge your abilities? Do you distract yourself all day with tv, video games, social media, or substances to avoid listening to your inner talk?

◎ **For two days, write about each day's inner talk/chatter experience.**

◎ **What have you observed about your inner talk/chatter?**

seeing red.

Click-click. Can you hear it steadily approaching? Click. It's the Red Pen and it's heading straight for your masterpiece. Are you momentarily traumatized when asked to fill a blank page with words? Do you suddenly see Red? Those markings across your sixth grade papers have scarred your future. Our dedicated teachers may have unknowingly bludgeoned our creative expression forever with that darn ballpoint pen.

At age 5, you got a cookie for coloring inside the lines. At age 6, you got gold stars when you hung the periods properly. But, at age 12 you were scolded with X's and not-happy faces because you used too many exclamation points and failed to stop your sentences from running wild. By age 16, you started to get the hang of perfection—anything to avoid Red. So now when it's time to get WiLD and creative, you fidget under your desk. Beady-eyes burn the back of your neck. Clicking echoes in your left ear. What if you do something wrong and that pen comes for you? **Splat:** *Too many commas! don't you need a dash? a hyphen? a Capital? a semi-colon? my-my your spelling is atrocious—how old are you again? they let you graduate from University?*

Before I go on, I need to confess. In 2003, during my first year as a classroom teacher, I graded with The Red Pen. (I just ducked.) Let me explain.

Feeling conflicted about it, I switched to a black pen. My special needs class of 4th, 5th, and 6th graders presented academic functioning below their grade level. I told them I wasn't a fan of circling and drawing arrows all over their papers in red ink. I thought it demeaning, and I didn't want to blunt their writing confidence any more than the "system" had already done. To my surprise, the kids wanted the Red feedback, complaining they couldn't tell my black pen from their pencil writing. We took a poll, and every student voted RED. So, I slid the red Bic back into my ponytail.

I tried an experiment and bought boxes of red pens for the students to correct their own papers. Instead of receiving my blood markings, I let them over-see their writing and initiate the edits. They felt empowered instead of judged. I also gave writing assignments to be completed with The Red Pen, no black ink and no pencil. I hoped both experiments would take the sting away from the humiliation of seeing Red.

Back to the beady eyes, the clicking, and you. You're not in grade school. There's nothing you need to prove. Journaling WiLD is not a space for judgment nor does it reward perfection. You are allowed to wander, discover, uncover, and declare in your journal. Lay your words across the page any way you wish. Let your Voice come through. You're free. Do you hear that? It's silence. No more click-click.

underwear.

My client has a precocious five year old. He's been choosing his outfits since he was four. His parents see no issue that his green top does not match his purple shorts, nor do they fuss if his socks aren't from the same set. Though some might place stronger parameters around how he chooses his wardrobe, I believe the autonomy teaches their son to be confidently creative and trust his decisions. He is being tamed to *stay* wild and pure.

However, there is one garment his liberal parents do not leave to their son's discretion: the underpants. They must be clean. Sound familiar? Of course, it does. Aren't you wearing clean underwear right now? Don't answer. Not sure why I asked.

You might wear the same jeans three days in a row. You might wear your socks two days in a row. But because it was drilled by every parent on earth, I bet you were conscious about putting on clean underwear today. And the reason why our parents cautioned us to wear clean undies is simply ridiculous. They didn't want the medics to think we weren't conscientious about our hygiene if, by chance, we got rushed into surgery after, I don't know, getting plowed down by a tractor or a speeding Corvette. Well, let me free you from your dirty underwear insecurity. If you should ever get injured by a rabid car, tractor, or flying saucer-thingy, it's likely the surgeons **won't** be interested in analyzing your undergarments (even if you are wearing the same underpants you wore yesterday).

94

Wear any underwear you want when you journal WiLD. You have permission. You don't have to keep your journal entries clean either. You don't have to make your entries pretty or conscientious, organized, perfect, positive, or acceptable. You are free to write messy, weird, wrong, and lopsided. You can scribble, scratch, misspell, and be angry in your journal. You are free to dress your journal up or down. You get to choose how your journal looks, feels, and sounds. Trust your uniqueness. You get to choose.

No one needs to know, read, someday discover, or ever get one inkling about what you've decided to record in your personal journal.

I mentioned earlier that somebody "found" my extremely well-hidden journal. I'm talking about that pink diary with faint paisley print, my first private book. That incident ruptured my trust for years. I feared putting my emotions and personal stories into writing. It took an act of rebellion to bring me back to keeping a private diary again. High school.

The person who found it didn't feel good about what I wrote. I didn't deliberately aim to slam, hurt, or punish anyone by what I wrote in my pink diary. They were **my** fourth grade thoughts. They were for me, not anyone else. I needed a place to sort them, meet-up with the corresponding feelings, integrate them, and find resolutions for my pain. I needed to connect my dots and source my WiLD. I wrote to escape, to daydream, to make-believe.

Because of that incident, I lost my freedom. I disguised myself into stories about other people. I let the characters ask my questions, try-on the answers, and confess for me. If you are in a predicament where privacy is a concern, you might have to open your mouth. Tell your loved ones or housemates to respect your PRIVATE journals.

Inside the front jacket of my journals I write: *This sacred book belongs to Michelle Bernard. It is for Michelle Bernard's eyes only. Please close this book if you are not ...* You get it.

I have considered writing: *This book is for Michelle Bernard's eyes only and if your eyes even skim over one of these pages, be very afraid. Because if I find out, you can consider your eyes...*
Just kidding—but I'm tempted.

I live alone now, so I don't have to warn or damn anyone to hell for disrespecting my privacy. But when I lived with others, I made it clear not to open my private book. And be sure that I informed them about the time when my journal was violated and that it's a shady breach to commit. People will usually show respect when you help them understand your needs. If you still feel threatened by a lack of privacy, keep your journal online. I'll discuss online journals during *craving paper*.

Your journal entries are privy to your eyes only. You can write anything you wish in them. In fact, I suggest you write everything. Be WiLD.

WiLD abandon.

The fundamentals of writing have been branded into your knuckles since you held your first #2 pencil. Mine, too. For thirty years I feared exclamation points and never dared try a semi-colon. Listen, the rules of proper writing wield little to no power when you're journaling WiLD, so take a breath. I proclaim: Let grade "A" grammar and structure decompose in your compost. Okay, that was harsh. But seriously, you will never be free to explore your Self if you hang your conscious mind on when to write *they're, their* or *there*.

Send your inner scholar and her wooden ruler to the principal's office. Don't write for anyone other than yourself. Write to see, hear, and declare yourself without bounds.

Discard perfect writing when it hinders you from flowing out your truth. **Writing what's true is more important** than how you write it.

Please abandon these rules so you can write WiLD.

I. ~~WRITE CERTAIN STUFF~~
II. ~~WRITE A CERTAIN WAY~~
III. ~~WRITE ONLY~~
IV. ~~WRITE DATES ON EACH ENTRY~~

abandon rule I

~~WRITE CERTAIN STUFF~~

How about no? Write any stuff you want.

You are free to explore WiLD authenticity.

Write for an audience of one, the important one.

You have authority over the content you choose to include in your journal.

I'd better write nice things, just in case....

I'd better say smart things, just in case...

I'd better not expose anything negative, mean, sad, or weak just in case the boogey-monster of law of attraction comes after me.

Nonsense.

No one will read your journal, so no one will judge it, score it or criticize it. No one needs to see it. Ever. Your words and emotions belong to you and you have a right to say and feel however you wish. You can write everything that is true, especially the truths you're not able to tell other folks. You can write your dark shit and tell your journal big goals that others might critique. Write your secrets and your yearnings. Brag about your triumphs.

In fact, the more YOU you put on the pages, and the more you write about your successes and challenges, the more you will awaken your Interior Voice.

abandon rule II

~~WRITE A CERTAIN WAY. WRITE LONGHAND SENTENCES LIKE YOU LEARNED IN SCHOOL~~

In school you wrote *complete sentences* to give your writing universal understanding.

You are not writing for the universe. Your journal is for you.

Employ WiLD acceptance.

You don't have to write properly or be scholarly, if you don't want to. Write your entries using complete sentences, run-on sentences, fragments, or use bullets and one-liners. Sprinkle single words all over the page and use hearts to dot each "i". Set yourself free. Every style of expression is acceptable. Create pretend words. Use all CAPS. Eliminate punctuation. Dabble in any style of writing that expresses your thoughts and feelings in the moment without editing.

abandon rule III

~~WRITE ONLY~~

Are you kidding? Because you are practicing WiLD acceptance, **you are free to express yourself using a WiLD array of markings.**

Write, draw, doodle, use symbols, stretch the letters to change their shapes. Use bubble lettering or stylized fonts. Enter your thoughts and feelings in a way that suits your WiLD authenticity.

Write with a red pen, colored pencil, crayon, marker, or watercolors. Write entries in shapes or in a spiral. Write around the perimeter of the page. Glue magazine pictures, words or objects into your journal. Write on the lines, between them, or diagonally over them. Break boundaries.

I created a series of *mostly blank book journals* called **the black coffee series**. There are inspirational blurbs on the sides and tops of pages. They do not define the page limit.

I encourage WiLD journalers to write over them, around them, or add to them. Doodle into them, frame them in doodle art. Do whatever. WiLD abandon breaks you from the confines of *I-hope-I-do-this-right.*

Breaking rules breaks your mind away from internal and external judgment.
This opens the gateway for your Interior Voice to speak.

abandon rule IV

~~DATE YOUR ENTRIES~~

Do it, if you want. If you don't, don't. There are other ways to time-stamp your entries. Use a **WiLD archival system**. Go beyond traditional ways of dating. (I promise this isn't a relationship book.)

Because journaling is a record of your life, I suggest you use some type of labeling system. You could label your entries:

1. Using the day of the week, i.e., MONDAY
2. By month, i.e., July
3. With a day in a series of days, i.e., day FIVE or week 18
4. By season, i.e., Summer
5. Or mix any combination from above, i.e., AUTUMN Saturday

My **WiLD archival system**: I write the month, day, and year on the inside jacket of each new journal. I write the day of the week at the top of my entries.

In school, we lost points if we didn't put our name, date, and subject on the page. I know. I was a school teacher. Non-traditional time-stamping works just as well. Be WiLD and time-stamp anyway you choose.

hands are for... writing

For the following exercises, **untamed** and **WiLD** are used interchangeably.

This exercise will tap your memory (PROGRAM) and stimulate your imagination (POSSIBILITY).

A *WiLD Tomato* is journaling untamed for 25 minutes at a time.

Francesco Cirillo created The Pomodoro Technique to minimize distraction and increase productivity. Activities are chunked into 25-minute blocks of focused attention. He used a kitchen timer shaped like a pomodoro tomato for the technique.

WiLD Tomato is a nod to The Pomodoro Technique.

You can set a timer on your microwave, phone, Alexa, or use your tomato timer.

Untamed journaling for 25 minutes AKA the *WiLD Tomato*

◎ Pick **one conversation starter** (journal question) from below,
and journal about it for 25 minutes—write a WiLD Tomato.

- **How did you help or support a peer/friend during your youth?**
- **Besides a parent, who was your greatest positive role model or influencer during your youth?**
- **How did your favorite musicians/entertainers influence your high school experience?**

For each **WiLD Tomato** you can write about what happened, where you were, how you felt, who was involved, what it influenced, and what changed.

✦

Untamed journaling for 10 minute intervals AKA the *WiLD Cherry*

*(The word <u>cherry</u> in this exercise has nothing to do with Cirillo's chunking system.
I made up the **WiLD Cherry** 10-minute journal chunk.)*

◎ Pick **one conversation starter**. Journal for 10 minutes—a WiLD Cherry.

- **How do you calm yourself when you feel stressed?**
- **Describe one of your proudest moments within the last 5 years.**
- **If you could write a book about your life, what would be the title? What events of your life would you write about? Why?**

For each WiLD Cherry consider what happened, where you were or are, how you feel, who is involved, what/who is influenced, and what changes.

The *WiLD Tomato* and *WiLD Cherry* are not speed exercises.
The 25 and 10-minute blocks are simply to chunk out undistracted time for journaling.
You can write for longer than the specified time.

choke on nothing.

Errr...!
Where do I begin?
I don't know what to say today.

We usually feel this way when we have far too much to say. It's easy to spend three hours in a conversation with your best friend. You normally talk your co-worker's ear off at lunch then chomp a bit more back at your desks. For your Facebook thread, thoughts click off your fingers at a rapid-fire pace. Your thoughts keep you awake at night. Your mind is busy. You entertain 60,000 thoughts every day. You have thoughts, ideas, and dreams rushing up and down the freeway of your mind all the time, yet for your journal: low visibility. Whenever you have a hard time figuring out what to write in your journal it's usually because you're not use to slowing down and noticing <u>what</u> you're thinking.

If you don't know how to start writing, use your senses.
Write what you hear, taste, see, smell, or feel.

Write what you hear.
It's so quiet out here. On my terrace. Birds chirping. And whistling. The garbage trucks must be in the parking lot down the street. I hear metal doors opening. Today is cooler than

yesterday. I might need to put on socks. Think I might text Sarah today. We need to schedule time to go for a walk. I hope she can go Sunday morning. **I want to tell her about**...

There we go. That last sentence started the flow of the WiLD.

Write what you see.
No one smiles when they order. Looking down. No eye contact. Checking their phones. Scanning the code then checking facebook or texting or whatever. the girl doing the drinks just checked her phone. Do they get in trouble for that—we used to—I miss when I worked at hamburger hamlet. Great group. **It was better serving in the bar because**...

Did it again. Got the WiLD started.

Pay attention to what's happening around you. You will naturally make associations when you write what's in front of you. It will lead you to a thought, feeling, memory, or desire.

Don't push if nothing shows up.

Some mornings I need the inner quiet. I'm not going to make things up just to get words on my page. If journaling ever felt like a chore to me, I'd never recommend it to you. On days when my mind is neutral, I write for only a few minutes. I sip my iced coffee, stare out the window and write 400 words which takes about 10 minutes. A WiLD Cherry.
I make a few lists. I write my goals. Nothing else. It's okay.

The purpose of journaling WiLD is to spend time listening to yourself every day; to get to know and understand yourself. Some days it's fulfilling to stay somewhat quiet.

What should I do if I feel uncomfortable journaling about my feelings?—
I'm nervous to find out what's going on in my head—

I can hear your questions wrestling in the leaves out my window. You've made it thus far, my friend, which shows you're eager to discover more. One reason why you might have resisted journaling in the past is because some part of you knows you have a shit-ton of unresolved feelings you're not ready to confront. **If this is you, it's likely you are enormously powerful.** But I understand your reservation. However, once you begin to sand, de-clutter, and buff your shine, there'll be no way you'll wanna dull your awareness again.

Let's examine resistance.
1. What if I see something within myself that scares me?
2. What if I admit something that triggers my life to change and that change affects others around me?

1. What if I see something within myself that scares me?
Perhaps there's stuff you're afraid to remember. Not because a boogey monster lurks within that stuff. Nothing inside you has reason to harm you. It's just information. Most of it wants to

protect you. Sometimes we're afraid to look into our thoughts because our Interior Voice knows that we'll see something that makes us feel compelled to change. The change might set other transitions into motion. Change can be uncomfortable.

Fearing **discomfort** might make you want to avoid journaling. Avoidance sounds like this:
I don't have time to journal.
I don't have anything to say.
I don't feel ready.

Discomfort is often the precursor for a big leap into more fulfillment, so welcome it. Offer Discomfort a chair, a warm drink, and a pen. If you feel uncomfortable about what you write, you are going to benefit the most.

Discomfort doesn't have to be synonymous with pain. Journaling WiLD is like stretching. Think about improving your flexibility. Tight muscles hurt a little when they are stretched, at first. There's a bit of pullback from the stuckness. Breathing and moving slowly helps diminish the discomfort. The results of regular, slow stretching include improved circulation, a wider range of motion, and reduced pain. Journaling is like stretching.

Whenever you choose to do or become something that, even meagerly, contradicts who you've been, you could feel uncomfortable. You might stop wanting what you want just to avoid the feeling. But with regular practice, regular stretching, you'll move beyond the stuckness and experience reduced pain and the circulation of life-affirming energy.

Feeling Determined? Enthusiastic? Irritated? Frustrated?

Your emotions either give you energy or deplete it. Love, Joy, and Contentment raise fulfillment and promote healing in your body. Despair, Bitterness, and Hate carry low vibratory energy. When they're experienced in excess, they depress energy and magnetize a life experience to match. If low vibratory emotions are left to fester, they'll contaminate the beliefs that shape your life.

No emotion is bad, wrong, or off-limit. All of your feelings are valid and worthy of expression, even the ones that calibrate low. As you journal, you'll bump into all of them, especially the emotions you'd rather avoid. Don't deny or push any feelings back into the darkness. There's a way to use your negative feelings to find fulfillment.

Thoughts reside in your mind and their corresponding feelings resonate in your body. When the two are experienced together often enough, they give birth to a belief. Your beliefs drive your choices. Beliefs can also alter your biochemistry. In short, your beliefs shape the way you experience your body and your life.

Since you have so many thoughts driving around every day, it's easier to know what you're believing by observing how you're feeling. If you catch yourself in a cycle of thinking it's nearly impossible to stop eating in the middle of the night, and if that thought makes you **feel** stressed, anxious, and ashamed because you're gaining weight despite exercising four times a week; that thought coupled with those feelings will eventually become anchored as the belief: *I can't lose weight no matter what I do.*

This belief drives you to skip gym appointments, keep a row of Ritz crackers under the driver's seat, and constantly remind your friends how much you hate your back-fat. Your beliefs have a Voice. They always speak. You can change any belief. To start, journal about how you feel.

Brain research shows you can become addicted to certain emotional states when you feel them **regularly and often.** Think of the feelings you favor. Let's do this together.

When something **amazing** happens to you, think of the emotion you usually feel. Get ready to write.

◎ Specifically, think about an amazing experience you *recently* had concerning a relationship with a partner or a friend. **How did you feel?** Perhaps you felt an Upbeat Emotion.

◎ Now go back in time. Remember something amazing that happened to you last year with a partner or a friend. How did you feel then? **Write the emotion you felt in your journal.** If two different emotions popped into your head, write them both in your journal.

Here's a collection of emotions to make your search easier. Choose or write your own.

anxious	tired	unglued	weepy	sluggish	scattered
strong	driven	defeated	determined	centered	stubborn
depressed	troubled	weak	dull	diligent	creative
energized	unwavering	bitter	confident	worried	under-whelmed
exhausted	focused	spirited	upset	aggressive	detached

courageous	purposeful	powerful	grateful	aware	aligned
ambitious	disillusioned	hopeful	scared	enthusiastic	engaged
passive	weary	healed	accomplished	apathetic	disappointed
awakened	joyful	guilty	lonely	bored	love
disengaged	hopeless	lively	sad	lazy	resentful
satisfied	unsatisfied	obligated	motivated	curious	undisciplined
ashamed	lost	hyped	irritated	angry	over-whelmed

Let's observe another feeling state. What emotion are you most likely to feel when **something you do not want** to experience happens?

◎ Remember something specific that you **did not** want to experience involving a partner or a friend. **How did it make you feel?** Perhaps, this is a Not-So-Upbeat Emotion.

Use the collection of emotions to jog your memory.

◎ **Have you ever felt that way before, under similar circumstances? Describe.**

Keep in mind, your brain wires around your habits of thinking and feeling. The emotion you feel **regularly and often** will eventually choose you (regularly and often).

Pause for a spell. Consider the two emotions that you feel **regularly and often**—one Upbeat Emotion and one **Not-So-Upbeat Emotion**. Most likely, it's the two you just wrote in your journal. Mine are.

My Upbeat Default Emotion (UDE): *Appreciation.*

I walk around the city saying *thank you* out loud when no one's around—well, they're around but not near me. Don't pretend you don't talk to yourself. I've seen plenty of folks speak to air. I'm not alone in this, am I? Or maybe it's more common for New Yorkers.

Anyway, writing my blessings is one of my journaling habits. Even when a situation in my life sucks, I ask my journal: *What could be good about this? How is this sucky event aligning me with my deeper desire?* I have a strong connection to Great Spirit, so being thankful is my automatic emotional reaction to most stuff that happens.

My Not-So-Upbeat Default Emotion (NSUDE— I added the word "So" because the acronym needed the S): *Disappointment.*

Disappointment has been my go-to response for just about every upsetting situation I've encountered: like when my beau in Chicago cheated on me with his best-friend and when my childhood friend banned all contact with me whenever her boyfriend was in town. Before I got the nerve to assert my Voice, I'd hide behind *disappointment;* then cry, eat, or nap. Besides feeling disappointed, I also felt rejected, dishonored, and de-valued. I wanted to be cherished and appreciated, yet I struggled to speak out and communicate these needs. *Disappointment* reigned. And letting it reign created a bigger problem: My NSUDE continued to feed the overarching belief—**I'm not valuable**—to my system.

Being addicted to your NSUDE can complicate your life. Once your NSUDE feels normal, and by normal I mean EXPECTED, your subconscious mind looks for ways to justify feeling it. Your NSUDE becomes attracted to you. It makes itself at home within you. (Awkward).

Your mind (PROGRAM) wants to avoid discomfort. Changing anything, even uprooting an uncomfortable emotion you've become addicted to, feels threatening to your subconscious PROGRAM.

To challenge my NSUDE I had to notice the *disappointment* whenever it came up and look under it to see if I was really feeling *rejected, devalued,* or *dishonored.* To feel valuable, I needed to, first, value myself by asking for what I wanted. This also meant I had to be willing to risk receiving an objection and, possibly, losing something. In my case, I risked losing certain relationships.

I journaled WiLD about the belief: **I am not valuable.** I "Listened" to how **I am not valuable** spoke in other areas of my life. It collided into business decisions, trespassed into love relationships, and sat in the pocket of a few more friendships. I made a decision to imagine myself being cherished, valued, and loved. I journaled the way I wanted these feelings to look and feel in my life. I did this **regularly and often** until my desired feelings felt comfortable.

Examine your NSUDE with your journal. See if it has something to show or tell you. Here's an example of how an NSUDE could surface for observation. I'm gonna use one of your possessions in this example. Something you own—like your purse. Wait. Let's not use your purse, because it probably contains your license, all your credit cards, and your keys. I'll use your shoes. You'll be glad I switched from your purse to your shoes when you read the rest of this.

Let's say you attend an event where you have to leave your shoes in the hallway—could be a yoga class, meditation gathering, a traditional Japanese dinner, or lunch in Hawaii. When you return after the event, one shoe is missing. You go into an itty-bitty tizzy, telling your buddy you're gonna leave a negative Yelp review when you get home.

You think your regular thoughts. *This always happens to me! Why did I trust these people to keep my shoes safe? I had a bad feeling about this. Of course I'm the only one missing a shoe.*

Your thoughts lead you to feel *irritated* during your Uber ride home because *irritation* is the NSUDE (Not-So-Upbeat Default Emotion) your brain and body has programmed. You journal about losing your shoe the next morning. You express *irritation* with no holds barred, pedal to the metal. You examine the beliefs you've written in your journal.

If something can go wrong, it will.
I am a magnet for bad luck.
I can't trust people.
I'm so irritated. This always happens to me.

Are there any realizations that can neutralize your NSUDE?

I got a ride home. I didn't have to walk 4 miles barefoot to my condo.
Keep writing.

The NSUDE comes up again: *But one of my shoes is still gone. Stolen!*
Write more.
I paid $89 for that pair of shoes. They weren't cheap. They were 3 years old and I already got substantial wear out of them. Those shoes made my feet swell after an hour. I have plenty more shoes at home. I don't really miss that small shoe so much. I'm gonna get another pair, one size up. Red, this time. Maybe it's good I finally got rid of those painful shoes.

Your NSUDE uncovered what you were believing though: *If something could go wrong, it will. I am a magnet for bad luck. People can't be trusted.*

When you experience an emotion that doesn't feel good or feels disempowering, one that stresses you out or makes you feel sick; instead of concluding—*This always happens to me* or *I'm a magnet for crap luck*, ask questions. Make a choice about what you'd rather feel.

What am I thinking about that makes me feel this way?
When have I felt this feeling before? or Does this belief show up in other areas of my life?
How would I rather to feel? What do I need to think and believe to feel the way I'd rather feel?
Your journal lets you step back and ask what else your feelings can show and tell you.

Instead of giving your NSUDE power over you, examine what it might reveal about you.

2. I might admit something that triggers my life to change, and that change might affect the people in my life, i.e., rock the boat at home.

Journaling about your family's values and obligations, including beliefs around eating, activities, money, illness/wellness and other lifestyle choices, can make you feel guilty if you harbor conflicting desires.

The person or people with the strongest influence over you have provided downloads into your subconscious program. That's just the way programming works. If you don't like the programming, you might feel they are to blame for contaminating your thoughts. You might fear that if your journal confronts the unwanted messages or beliefs learned from your loved-ones, it will damage your relationship with them.

No one is to blame for the way you choose to think right now.

Your loving parents, guardians, and teachers were never focused on killing your vision, punishing you, restricting you, or squashing your power. They simply handed you their beliefs, standards, and opinions, whether good or otherwise, because of their desire to protect you. Remove the jury and the judge. Blame no one for anything.

You get to clarify your personal feelings and beliefs in your journal. Question whether your feelings and beliefs support your fulfillment. If they don't, decide if you want to change them. You have this choice. From now on, you get to imagine who you want to be. You can listen to the messages from your life and declare what you want to believe.

hands are for... writing, listening, and deciding

◎ What other emotions does your NSUDE make you feel?

◎ What can your NSUDE teach you about your needs and desires?

◎ How would you rather feel? Imagine feeling that way. Journal WiLD about it.

◎ What could you do to feel the way you'd rather feel?

Journaling **WiLD** is

untamed **W**riting to **i**magine, **L**isten, and **D**eclare.

Journal with WiLD abandon.

I. Explore WiLD authenticity

II. Employ WiLD acceptance

III. Express yourself with a WiLD array of communicative markings

IV. Use a WiLD archival system

craving paper?

I was having one of those mornings. My fingers were dancing so fast over the keys, I was sure I'd missed some clicks. I was journaling in the app, Evernote, while riding the train into Manhattan. The conductor asked for my ticket, the only reason I looked up.

"Good morning. You're writing again."
"Uh-huh," I kinda-smiled. If I stayed long in a conversation, my fingers would lose the messages. They needed me to keep speaking.
The train slowed into Penn Station. I didn't jump into line like everyone else. I pressed out a few more words, slipped my iPad back into my bag, and hung my gaze where the last sentence left me. The conductor must have been watching the whole time.
"Gee, you were really into that!"

I imagined what he'd witnessed. I probably looked like someone who'd been starved then set loose to devour the digital plate.

He had no idea, but my morning journal entry had transported me to a jungle treehouse in Costa Rica where I let my legs dangle from the bamboo floor. Mango nectar pooled between my fingers as I pulled back the flesh to take a bite. He had no idea that seconds ago I was lounging in a hammock, drinking coconut water straight from the shell. The music of the rainforest over-powered the squeal of the NJ transit train pulling into Penn Station.

"Yes, I usually get sucked into the stuff I'm writing," I told him.

It wasn't the first time that conductor chuckled when I left the train.

I have years and pages of journal entries saved in Evernote. Those entries are saved to the Cloud, so I don't have to shelve another journal or worry about hiding my private book from sneaky eyes. There are benefits to paper and pen journal entries like writing at an angle, doodling, and using artistic symbols. In paper and pen entries, my penmanship might change to match the person whose opinion or advice is responsible for the thought I'm writing. Your hand-writing can channel the Voices within you as well as the Voices that aren't your own. It's been helpful to see my real handwriting when I'm working to shave away outer influences and get to the purity of my own thoughts.

I prefer to journal the old-fashion way, paper and uni-ball pen, but I always use digital journaling when I travel. Tech innovators have sympathized by creating journaling apps that let you write on your screen with a stylus. Much appreciated.

in the clouds.

I'm somewhat of a collector—of gadgets. I have three iPods, three MacBooks, one 15 year old Dell PC, and an android cell phone. Oh, I almost forgot the iPad! I'm sure you are a collector, too. When you own a buttload of these devices you need to designate a drawer to hold their cords and adapters. It also means you could press pause on acquiring more physical stuff and let your gadgets hold your private book. Store your journal in your digital space. It's more convenient than building shelving units to keep your overflow of leather bound journals.

Evernote is my preferred journaling app. There's also 750words.com , an app you can program to send yourself a reminder to write. Seven hundred and fifty words equals three pages, enough to meet Julia Cameron's liking. Your pages are locked behind a password, perfect if you need privacy. Other online journals I recommend can be found at diaroapp.com, dayoneapp.com, and penzu.com.

Most online journaling apps, including Evernote, require a monthly or yearly subscription to get the extra benefits like unlimited space, cloud storage, on and offline accessibility, photo posting, and audio recording.

press record.

I use my audio journal when my ideas are flowing and I don't have time to sit or a pen to write. It's also an option if you don't have the use of your hands for writing. I time-stamp my audio entires. I also title and catalog them, because I record them at random. Your vocal inflections are saved in recordings, so you can listen to the real-life tone of your feelings during playback.

You can substitute daily paper journaling with daily audio journaling. Just follow WiLD abandon rules and record your entries without censoring or premeditating what you "should" say.

One difference with audio journaling is: **DO listen to the playback of your depressing audio entries at least one time within a week of recording them.** One to two playbacks are plenty. The emotion sounding through your voice during playback will powerfully affect your PROGRAM. Your Interior Wisdom will have an immediate response to these audio recordings. After you playback your *blue audio* entries, journal a hand-written or typed response. Audio journaling helps discharge sour emotions. The written response to your audio will bring you clarity by letting you examine what your NSUDE wants to reveal to you.

You can use audio journaling for any of the WiLD offerings coming up in guide*line* four.

make a sandwich.

I used to wake up every morning by 7:30 am. I lived in Harlem then, only 20 minutes to mid-town by subway. I'd shower and dress fast as a superhero to make it to the A train, arriving for my first client with 10 minutes to spare. Jeepers. The rushing. It wouldn't have to feel so brutal if I would just wake up 30 minutes earlier!

My workout buddy at the time, a corporate attorney who spent long hours at her office, rose by 5 am every day. She'd complete her morning routine which included inspirational reading, meditation, and a workout at my gym before going to her office.

5 am! Aren't you tired? How do you do it, girl?
Getting up early was her answer to accomplishing more in a day. She'd gotten used to it.

I could never do that. I swore against it, though secretly, I wished for her body clock.
To get out of bed by 5 am, *oh the places I'd go...*

At that time, waking by 7:30 am felt like I'd hadn't slept at all. I was insane to believe 5 am could improve my day. Be careful what you swear against (or wish for in secret).

When I moved to New Jersey, I had no choice but to wake up early. **4:30 am early.** My Manhattan appointments were booked at 8. After one week, I loved it.

Three fewer hours of sleep, and I was less tired than when I slept later. Seems I liked (needed) contemplative mornings. I created a morning routine to maximize my (surprisingly new) natural rhythm.

Let the dogs out to run and pee in the backyard. 4:30.
Pour iced coffee in the goblet. Sit and stare. 4:45.
Shower + play inspirational videos. 5
Hop on the train for the city. 5:30-ish. The -ish represents the delays. (Many mornings I'd stare down a dark track with my fingers crossed).

Back to my morning routine...
Write in my digital journal on that train. 5:40
I wrote every day for 30 minutes. Afterward, I'd read my Kindle.
Waking up earlier wasn't a burden at all. The extra time created space to fit a hearty journal sandwich. Be careful, your wish could improve your life!

What time of day will you journal WiLD? Mornings in the bagel shop? During your commute? After work in the cafe beside the gym? In the bathtub after dinner? In bed after Dancing with the Stars?

Make your journal sandwich.

Journaling WiLD lasts 10-25 minutes. Sandwich journaling WiLD in-between two other activities that are already fixed into your daily routine. Say, you brew your tea or coffee in the morning then look through emails before breakfast. Checking emails takes about 25 minutes because it involves clicking on links, shooting out replies, and getting lured over to Facebook. After your email shenanigans, you go back upstairs to shake your daughter because she always manages to sleep through her alarm blasting Bruno Mars.

Where can you sandwich journaling WiLD?

If you shave away the 25 minutes of email checking and Facebook scrolling, you could sandwich journaling WiLD between getting your coffee and waking your girl. Ah, that means quiet, peaceful, *me time* for you every morning. Plus, you'll begin your day without carrying the baggage of suppressed feelings and muddled clarity. Skip futzing around the internet, plugging your energy into other people's random needs, opinions, and rants; and journal your own WiLD needs, opinions, and rants.

Or maybe you'd rather sandwich journaling into your nighttime routine. If you bathe in Epsom salts and essential oils after dinner then read to your boys in bed, you can journal WiLD while you wait for the tub to fill. Sandwich journaling WiLD between bathing and reading.

Here's my current journal sandwich.

I walk my pups, then journal for 25 minutes with a goblet of iced coffee. After journaling, I listen to inspirational speakers on YouTube while I shower. Journaling WiLD is sandwiched between my coffee and an inspirational shower.

Your journal sandwich will help you maintain a **daily ritual** of WiLD. I recommend journaling at the same times everyday. If you can't journal daily, journal on the same days and times each week.

Make your sandwich a ritual. Bon appetit.

hands are for... writing

Make your journal sandwich.

◎ **Write out your morning or evening or mid-day routine and sandwich journaling WiLD between two activities already fixed in your schedule.**

WiLD is untamed **W**riting to **i**magine or visualize, **L**isten, and **D**ecide or **D**eclare.

elements of Journaling WiLD

- Write every day or on specific days as a ritual. Make a journal sandwich.

- Write untamed. Write what's on your mind. Tell your truth. Don't censor. Be raw. **Practice WiLD abandon.**

- Journal daily. Pick a WiLD Tomato (25 minutes of free-writing) or a WiLD Cherry (10 minutes of free-writing). If nothing comes to mind, write what's right in front of you or **use an offering from guide*line* four.** Use a digital or audio journal whenever you want.

- Your **Interior Voice is allowed** to speak, question, answer, imagine, decide, and declare when you write. Give every part of your Self a Voice. Let your prickly, knotted, surly inner Troll-Gnome whine. Let your magical Child Self play pretend. Let your Wise Self spill the T (Truth).

- You don't have to re-read every entry you've written to be able to hear your Voice. **You'll be able to Listen to your Voice as you write.**

go beyond

It's not about what you deserve.
It's about what you believe.

WONDER WOMAN, the movie

guide*line* four : explore WiLD.

I get a bare-bones look at my choices and my fears. when I journal, I weigh what I could do, decide what I will do, untangle myself from what I've decided to let go of, and make peace with my choices.

May these WiLD offerings penetrate your life and fill your missing peaces (not misspelled).

These seven journaling offerings will let you hear your Interior Wisdom, solve particular problems, and clarify your beliefs. The offerings illuminate self awareness so you can declare to become the person you imagine you can be. Spend between 10-25 minutes in each journal session.

7 WiLD journaling offerings

- *what if...*
- *all about me*
- *POSSIBILITY journaling*
- *between you and me*
- *the hungry heart exercise*
- *conversation starters*
- *the awakening*

Put your dreams on a pedestal.

Focus on them.
Live into them.
Become them.

offering #1

what if...

You've had it. Why is it so hard to meet a nice, single guy? You're fed up with dieting only to gain all the weight back when summer ends. Will you ever finish your book? Is a second home in the Berkshires too much to ask for? You want these things. You've wanted them for years, but you're getting to the point where *wanting* has done nothing to make them happen. Even the affirmations you wrote into bubbles at that New Year's Eve meet-up haven't popped into your reality, yet. Maybe you're not supposed to meet a guy, stay lean, write a book, or live in a dream home. Maybe it's not in your stars. Ugh! You're tempted to scream obscenities, but the kids are in the car.

Flash ahead two years, and what? You've let your doubt about the struggle to fulfill these dreams marinate in your mind and your body. Now you've cemented a PROGRAM, an unconscious attachment to these doubtful thoughts and feelings. Give it a little more time and you'll be fully addicted to doubting these dreams are possible. By then, you'll defend your doubt and resist your dreams. If you get to a point when you believe your dream is impossible, you're gonna be right. Your beliefs penetrate your life.

Stop. All is not lost. Even if a dream has taken a long while to become fulfilled, you don't have to give up believing in it. You must let your subconscious PROGRAM see it happening. Suggest your dream to your subconscious PROGRAM by using a *what if* question.

Use a *what if* question for the desires you've felt are nearly impossible to receive, the desires you fear you're not ready to receive, and/or the desires you have no idea how to make happen.

What if you were weeks away from meeting your life-partner?
What if you were two sizes smaller by Thanksgiving?
What if there was an estate available for a lesser amount than usual in the Berkshires?
What if the next client you took on introduced you to the publisher for your book?
What if a new friend lived in the neighborhood you're about to move to?

Breathe possibility into your goals by using *what if* questions, and revive your life.

Use a *what if* question instead of an affirmation. If your PROGRAM, your subconscious data, doesn't agree with an affirmation, it'll chuck it out the car window.

For example, if your affirmation states: *I'm going to meet my husband this year.*
But the evidence in your PROGRAM or an inner belief says: *I haven't been on a good date in two years. It's so hard to meet a good man.*
Here's how you'll behave based on the belief from your PROGRAM: *You aren't friendly to the men who innocently say Hello, because you don't trust their intentions. You aren't relaxed on dates because you're busy looking for flaws and inconsistencies. You constantly tell your girlfriends how awful men are.*
Your beliefs always affect your behavior. It will be difficult to make a love connection acting this way.

Affirmations get vetoed when your PROGRAM doesn't find any evidence to back them up.

If your affirmation states: *At the next networking event, I will meet a publisher for my book.*

But evidence from your PROGRAM contradicts: *Publishers don't have time to talk to every person who wants to write a book.*

Your behavior will align with your belief: *Instead of mingling at the networking event, you stand close to three of your co-workers and talk about how much you hate networking. You hear there's a publisher from Hay House talking to a small group in the back. You go over to listen but do not give the lady a card or tell her anything about your finished manuscript at home.*

If your affirmation states: *I will maintain my summer weight for the whole year.*

But the evidence in your PROGRAM contradicts: *I have never kept my summer weight all year. It's hard for my body to stay lean. It's probably because weight gain runs in my family. I get hungrier in the winter anyway. Everybody does.*

Your behavior will align with your belief: *You munch on gobs of pretzels and white cheese popcorn after work and gain four pounds by September. You blame the change of season. By October, you only go to the gym once a week instead of five. You stash a big bag of M&M's in your top drawer after Halloween.*

Your beliefs will always penetrate your life. Your beliefs are imprinted in your PROGRAM. Your PROGRAM is responsible for 85% of your behavior. Your PROGRAM responds to the data and IMAGERY it has stored. If you want to experience a desired outcome, you'll need to influence your PROGRAM with specific data and imagery aligned with that outcome.

To get your PROGRAM onboard with your goal, declare your desired outcome using a *what if* question, then imagine the *what if* until it feels real.

Your PROGRAM responds to pictures more than words. Visualizing your goals *regularly and often* will affect the way you behave, speak, listen, declare, and believe.

Here are the *what if's* I've used to move (scary) desires from my crossed fingers into real-life experiences.

What if I'm able to pay off all my debt after I move to New York City?
What if I could teach high school theatre?
What if I get special mention in the bodybuilding show?
What if I could afford to live in a one bedroom apartment in Manhattan?

All of the *what if's* above manifested into my real life, but their outcomes were magnified beyond what I asked for or imagined.

☑ I paid off all my debt within 6 months of moving to Manhattan, and saved enough money to vacation twice a year.

☑ I won first place in my first **and** second bodybuilding shows.

☑ I was appointed Head of the Theatre Department and given a $33,000 budget within two months of teaching in a new school.

☑ I lived in several one-bedroom apartments in Manhattan working full-time as an artist and teacher.

Here are the *what if* questions I'm journaling about right now.

What if I lived and worked from a houseboat for 6 months?
What if I bonded happily with a forever partner?
What if I could empower women around the world to make themselves available to fulfillment in every way?
What if I lived in Costa Rica and spoke fluent Spanish?
What if I could be counseled by a shaman?

Can you imagine how these *what if's* will look when they get magnified?

mental movies.

Your PROGRAM responds to your imagination more than your words. Visualize your *what if's*.

Visualizing is like playing a movie in your mind. Have you seen the movie, Jaws? See yourself on that boat with Roy Schneider, Richard Dreyfus, and Anthony Quinn hunting a shar..., nah; I change my mind. Don't pretend you're lost at sea on a fishing boat with two guys and one masochist, being stalked by a killer shark that's likely to eat you, because it eats everyone. Can we agree it might be better to visualize something that makes you wanna dance instead of feel freaked out?

Picture yourself walking behind the Pink Ladies to the graduation carnival for Rydell High. The football field is sprawling with festivities: tea cup rides, strongman bells, cream pies on faces for prizes. Rizzo and Kenickie are making out on the ferris wheel. Danny is wearing a milky white sweater with a large R stitched into the bottom left pocket. Sandy has found a shiny pair of black leggings, a biker jacket, and open-back heels.

Her blonde curls bounce but hardly behave. She smashes her cigarette under her toe, sending Danny into song. Can you see all this? If you've seen Grease with John Travolta and Olivia Newton John, you probably can. Pretend you're there. You are on that Rydell High School field. Even if you haven't seen Grease, the movie, you can imagine the scene from the description. You just visualized Grease. Imagine your *what if's* the same way.

Practice with the following *what if's*. See all the details like your mental movie is real. Here are *what if's* for a body goal. Read each and imagine yourself living the *what if* in reality.

what if I had sculpted legs?
what if my belly was flatter?
what if I loved vegetarian meals?
what if I felt comfortable seeing my body in a full-length dressing room mirror?

You can use a *what if* question to imagine your desired career, romance, health, financial state, social life, or any personal situation. Write and imagine your *what if's* **regularly and often** and your PROGRAM will get onboard to help you realize them.

If changing your belief about something you desire to have, be, or do has been a consistent downer, raise your belief by journaling with *what if* questions.

Use offering #1:

To write yourself into your goal.

To see yourself from a different perspective.

To solve a problem.

To make a decision.

To make a change.

When you're going through a renewal, for example, a new job or new relationship status.

Note: *what if* questions can be used in conjunction with POSSIBILITY journaling in offering #3.

hands are for... imagining

◎ Write 6-8 *what if* questions every day <u>for a week</u>.

You can add new *what if's* every day or write the same ones over and over. Each day add sentences to expand your *what if* questions with details and descriptions. Elaborate until you've expanded your *what if's* to paragraphs or whole pages of description. Pause and imagine each *what if,* picturing the details.

Notice how your *what if's* change your relationship to your goal.

After you finish the exercise above, make it a habit to write then imagine your *what if's* two or more times a week to connect your PROGRAM to your goals.

if the noise outside

gets too loud

how will you ever hear your Self?

better to write Her

draw Her

scribble Her onto a napkin and stick Her in your purse.

carry Her with you everyday.

She needs to know you want to hear from Her.

She needs to know you care or She'll crawl away and sleep

head under the pillow

offering #2

all about me

Getting feedback from your Interior Voice.

Have you ever given advice to someone, paused and thought:
Hmmm, that was good—where did that come from? I ought to listen to myself more often.
Yes. I agree.

People who need people are the luckiest people in the world. Barbra Streisand sang these lyrics in the movie, Funny Girl. Though it sounded true, it took me years to understand why. Through social interactions, you're able to experience compatibility as well as contrast. You get to see who you are and who you aren't. Connecting with others lets you listen and be heard. It gives you opportunities to practice loving and accepting those who are like and unlike you.

No man is an island. It's hard to survive in total isolation. In the movie Castaway, Tom Hanks befriends a volleyball, Wilson, so he doesn't have to be alone with his thoughts. Solitary confinement is a punishment in prisons. Without social interaction, we risk depression and delusion. We need each other.

So it's understandable that you want to share your ideas, plans, and goals with somebody else. You want to converse with your buddy before you go into contract for the 3-bedroom townhouse. You need to talk to your bestie before you move in with your boyfriend and his mom. You want to consult your pops on whether you should renovate the bathrooms first or do the kitchen. You want feedback. You want support regarding your decisions. You want validation. This is expected. People need people.

Yet, you are wiser than you realize. Consider consulting yourself for feedback and support.

These days we're overloaded with feedback. The cell phone stays glued to our eyes. The inter-web is stuffing you with imagery and opinion until you're overweight with confusion. Social media tells you what to think and do (inject your booty and your lips or no one will look at you), cookies tells you what you want (you left those red cowboy boots in your cart, darling), online gurus give you contradictory answers (eat butter, don't eat butter). These days you could use a little solitary confinement just to remember who you are.
Journal to the rescue.

The *all about me exercise* is a consultation with your Internal Wisdom.

With the *all about me* journal offering, the feedback comes from YOU. Actually, you get feedback **from a perspective** within you. Did that sound really out there? Don't panic. I'm not getting woo-woo right now. Okay, I am.

You are a complex individual, can we agree? There are aspects of you, archetypes as Carl Jung calls them, that make up the "characters" in your Person. Each archetype has a viewpoint. Generally, they all want to protect you. Your archetypes, or Interior Voices, derive their viewpoints from the data in your PROGRAM, and they also formulate ideas from your POSSIBILITY mind, a portal that stores All Potentials.

They know everything about you. *They* meaning the aspects of YOU. Stay with me...

You can inquire from your Angel Self, your inner Muse, your Gnome Self, your Future or Past Self, and God or your Higher Energy. *Ahhhh....!!* (Harps playing)
Are you feeling like Michelangelo right now, or am I projecting?

Listen, if you're not down with the idea of having the voice of *God* speak through you, substitute a different "feeling" like Truth, Power, Love, Higher Self, Allness, or if it makes more sense for you, let Oprah or Ellen speak. Whatever or whoever represents your highest energy is okay—or skip hearing from that particular messenger. Let the other aspects of your Interior Voice have their say.

Here's how to journal WiLD using the *all about me* exercise.
1. Decide who you'd like to hear from. There's a list below.
2. Write the question you want to examine in your journal.
3. Write the entire journal entry in the Voice you've chosen to hear from. Let your chosen Interior Voice answer the question and tell you what they believe.

Here's an example:

1. **Who:** *I'd like to hear from <u>my</u> **Mothering Self** (This is not your actual mother's Voice)*

2. **My question:** *Will you comfort me during this transition?*

3. **Sample journal entry from the Voice of my Mothering Self:** *Michelle, you are putting so much pressure on yourself. You've always been a determined child. I'm not asking you to change that quality. But I do think you'd benefit from pausing before bedtime, sipping tea, and reading a book. Honey, give your mind a rest.*

Michelle, I believe in your goals just as much as you. I want you to achieve everything you decide to go after. But it would be good for you to set aside time to stop striving, and enjoy stillness. I know you journal at the beginning of the day; try resting at the end of the day.

How 'bout tonight? Wrap up in a blanket and relax for an hour before bed. See how it affects your sleep. I'm pretty sure it'll rejuvenate you over the long run. Sit and breathe. Have you considered meditating before bed?

I've listened to my Gnome Self using this exercise. I've asked it about my singing career and let it tell me what it wanted to protect in regard to my love relationships. I've used this exercise to come to a level of acceptance and forgiveness concerning things that have puzzled me in life.

Your Interior Voices will provide guidance suited to your unique life experience, because the observations and answers come from an aspect of you.

The **hands are for...** exercise is coming up, but let me impart one last thing. When getting feedback from others, I certainly believe people do need people. Connecting with others is part of our purpose. But be aware to seek people who will fan the flames for your miracle, and be mindful to avoid folks who kindle your fears into a bonfire.

Pick "your people" like you pick your shoes. Make sure they fit or you're gonna be in pain.

Use offering #2:

To see a different perspective.

To forgive yourself.

To forgive someone or something.

To tap into your own wisdom.

To solve a problem.

To make a decision.

When you're going through a renewal, for example, a new job or new relationship status.

hands are for... listening

all about me

◎ Choose an Interior Voice you'd like to hear from. This Voice will respond in your journal entry.

◎ Write the question or topic you want to examine in your journal.

◎ Write the entry from the perspective of the Interior Voice you've chosen. Let the chosen Voice answer your question or respond to the topic.

Allow the Interior Voice to tell you their needs and beliefs regarding the question, as well as explain related thoughts and feelings they have about you.

Here is a list of possible Voices.

Higher Energy or God
Past Self
Child Self
Future Self
Gnome or Troll Self (saboteur)
Angel Self (protector, messenger)
Wise or Sage Self (wisdom)
Mothering or Fathering Self
Muse

what you move toward
will also move toward you.

I don't just mean WHAT YOU MOVE TOWARD using your feet.
I mean
using your feet,
your eyes,
your hands,
your words,
and your knowing.

come alive.

what expression of life are you moving toward?

imagine, speak, move, and touch the life you desire
or you'll die inside the plans everyone has for you.

offering #3

POSSIBILITY journaling

You don't need a crystal ball to see your future; not when you have a journal.

You have to be WiLD to practice POSSIBILITY journaling, but I know you are. You're curious and willful. During guide*line* three you put objects in your mouth to identify them, by golly. You haven't always been tamed. So, I know you won't be taken aback when I tell you that you'll use your imagination and pretend when you write your POSSIBILITY journal entries.

The "i" in WiLD stands for *imagine*. POSSIBILITY journaling is imagining or pretending you are living the outcome and experiencing the feeling you desire. I'll be using the words *pretend, imagine,* and *make-believe* to describe POSSIBILITY journaling.

Look at the word **make-believe**. Let the dash stand for **yourself**. **Make yourself believe**. Now attach **it's true** to the end. **Make yourself believe it's true**. This is what you'll do when you write your dreams and desires in your POSSIBILITY journal. If it still sounds outlandish, let me break the news. You're already **making yourself believe** all kinds of stuff **is true**. You pretend every day.

Have you watched folks play video games? Their bodies shift and twist to get away, through, and around the obstacle on the screen. For them, the unreal game experience is real. And how about television shows? Folks think they know the characters personally. They cry at

Luke and Laura's wedding and warn the Bachelorette to stay away from the dude with the temper. Only someone who has made herself believe the scenario in the tv box is real would do that. Folks play pretend when they shop. Your VISA is nearly maxed out, yet you imagine you've got Paris Jackson's wallet when you purchase the white leather jacket and matching thigh-high boots. This is **making yourself believe it's true** you can afford them. Pretending is a common practice among grown folks, even though it sounds childish. And it's obvious from these examples, **making yourself believe** (something is) **true** affects the way you behave in reality.

What if you chose to **make yourself believe** for things that could elevate your life experience?

What if you made yourself believe your body was healed? Would that change the way you talked about your health? Your body? Your future? What if you imagined relaxing with tea in the kitchen of the beach house you expect to own someday? Would that affect your blood pressure? Would it make you more disciplined about saving 10% of your paycheck? What if you made yourself believe you could be promoted to the corner office? Can you see it? Would it make you confident at work now? Would it inspire you to assert your opinion during the morning meetings? Imagine speaking on the TEDx stage, looking at a front row of smiling faces. Can you see yourself there? Does it make you inspired to finish writing your book?

Unfortunately, it's easier to make ourselves believe there's a target on our backs for the outcomes we do not want.

You're scheduled to speak to large group of parents at your daughter's high school this Friday. You wake up Tuesday with a slight cough. Frantically, you pop lozenges and hoard tea all day. You imagine how awful it could be if the cough turned into a 4-day sneeze-fest, shredding your vocal cords, leaving you hoarse and sleepless every night. You imagine your sinuses getting so stuffed that you sound like a baby seal. And worse, you think about these horrific outcomes all week long. You are **making yourself believe** you will be a complete mess by Friday, even though it's Tuesday and all you have is a cough.

Or you could *make yourself believe* another possibility. On Tuesday morning, while preparing lozenges and tea, you imagine eager moms listening to you present ideas that will make senior year memorable for the graduates. You hang your green dress on the closet door. It represents energy and optimism. Each night you tell your journal how you hope to inspire the parents and staff. As you write, you imagine yourself behind the podium; the administrative staff seated to your left, student counsel to your right. Your best friend, Amber, gives the thumbs up. You imagine looking out at the audience thinking *I'm so grateful to be here. I appreciate each one of you for coming.* Then you hear the applause. You see yourself speaking to parents during the reception that follows. One of them thanks you for volunteering to lead the Parent's Committee. She becomes a new friend.

How do you think you'd feel if you made yourself believe the first possible outcome? Maybe panicked, anxious, and defeated. These emotions would make your body tense, tired, and possibly, ill. Imagine how those emotions might affect your behavior on Friday.

How would you feel if you made yourself believe the second outcome?

Which possibility would you want to impress upon your subconscious PROGRAM, the part of mind that affects how you think, talk, feel, and act 85% of the time?

Your imagination can penetrate reality.

You always have the option to believe in any outcome. This is how you employ superconsciousness! **Use your POSSIBILITY journal to try-on your desired outcome.** Remember, the more you impress the picture of what you want onto your mind, the easier it is for your PROGRAM to get your body in motion to receive it.

POSSIBILITY journaling makes the unreal, real. Imagine what you want.

I use my POSSIBILITY journal once or twice a week. It has created miracles in my life, but I need to clarify something for you. My miracles did not come because I begged or pleaded for them in my journal. POSSIBILITY journaling affected my beliefs and changed my behavior so that I lived in a way that made me available to receive exactly, and sometimes, more than I imagined!

Use offering #3:
To feel motivated, inspired, or energized.
To generate ideas.
To change a belief.

To see a different perspective.

To tap into your own intuition.

To make a decision.

When you're going through a renewal, for example, a new job or new relationship status.

hands are for... imagining

POSSIBILITY journaling
Write yourself into your future.

◎ Choose two of your *5 parts of being* to focus on:
Finance, Career, Health, Relationship, and Spirituality.

◎ What specific feeling or outcome (goal) would you like to experience in real-life from two of your *parts of being*?

◎ Pretend you're experiencing these outcomes. Journal about where you are, what you're doing, and describe how it feels to live this outcome as real. You can describe what you see, taste, touch, hear, or smell. Use details that make it real.
Write a POSSIBILITY entry for each goal.

Write the entry as if it's going to happen or as if it has already happened.
Your body and mind will feel and believe your entry can happen for real.

Here's a snippet of a POSSIBILITY journal entry written as if <u>it's going to happen</u>. The *part of being* is **Career**: *This is such a special time for me. They are announcing the position soon. I prepared for three months to get this position. When I get to work, I notice the sticky note from my boss on top of a stack of folders.*
It reads: **Bring these to my office before lunch.**
When I set them down, she has a smile on her face. She asks if I'd feel overwhelmed putting a meeting together by Friday for my new staff. I almost scream. I got the position!

Here's a similar snippet of POSSIBILITY journaling written as if <u>it already happened</u>: *That day still stands out as one of the best in the last 10 years. When my boss asked me to visit her office before lunch, I had no idea she was going to tell me that I was the unanimous decision—the clear choice for Project Manager!!!! I had a feeling they would announce it sometime during the week, but not on Monday. That surprised me for sure.*
I used the rest of the week to organize my meeting notes into a speech. Plus, I treated myself to a new pant suit for Friday...

Your **what if** questions can be used to prompt POSSIBILITY journaling.

Additional exercise:
Review your **what if's**.

Choose 1 or 2 *what if's* to expand and describe with a POSSIBILITY journal entry.
Write the outcomes as if they will happen or already have happened.

offering #4

between you and me

A dialogue with your Self.

Don't Worry, Be Happy. Wait a minute, not so fast. I need more than a comma to move from yuck to bliss. The Bobby McFerrin melody from the 80's had everybody whistling about changing their emotional state at the snap of a finger. When I'm worried, frustrated, confused, or depleted I can't Pollyanna into *Happy* without a few emotional rungs in between. I need to neutralize my negative emotion first.

Between you and me is an internal dialogue between your Self and your Interior Self. You can use it to neutralize an uncomfortable emotion. You can also use *between you and me* to weigh a challenging decision or celebrate a courageous endeavor.

You get to speak to an aspect of your Interior Voice. These Voices are your archetypes. In essence, they are aspects of your Person. They symbolize universal patterns of thought and behavior according to psychologist, Carl Jung. Everyone has a Wise Self, Future/Past Self, Child Self, Mothering/Fathering Self, Gnome Self, Omnipotent Self, and others. Each archetype has needs and opinions that guide and protect you based on either the data recorded in your PROGRAM or the Infinite Potentials chosen by your POSSIBILITY mind.

Here's an example of neutralizing an emotion using the *between you and me* dialogue.

A dialogue between Myself and my Child Self.

Me: Been feeling lost. confused. I'm looking for you again. You were never confused about what you wanted.

Child Self: I'm here. Over here. I've been reading. And singing, too.

Me: Yeah. There you are. Glad I found you. I've been feeling so wishy-washy about my faith. You were never like that. when I was with you—I looked forward all the time. I've been looking back lately. feels troubling. not energizing.

Child Self: Yep. We used to dream on the bed. We'd fantasize, then play records and dance. We wrote stories, and most of the stuff we wrote about came true. We read books that took us on adventures.

Me: I know. I want to do that with you again.

Child Self: Yay! That was fun.

Me: But where should I start?

Child Self: Hey, that's easy. Put on your headset of tunes and let's go for walk. We'll imagine our future while we jam. What are you reading? Go find a good story. Fiction!!

Me: how come you don't lose hope—ever?

Child Self: I never think that my dreams might NOT happen. I know they will. Somehow. That's why I always act like they will. And I never stop dreaming!!! Or reading. Or believing. Never. Let's go for a walk, Michelle.

Here's an example of overcoming fear using the *between you and me* dialogue.

A dialogue between Myself and my Gnome Self.

Gnome: Thinking again? Damn, you're so intense. What are you chasing after now?

Me: I'm creating my life experience. clearly you can see that I'm making-believe and journaling and enabling my faith.

Gnome: Yeah, more hope. Aren't you tired of that crap? *Hope* sure does waste a lot of time **and money**. What a joke. Look at the money you've spent creating your "life experience". All those art supplies. They're piled to the ceiling. And books. No one wants to read your books. It's not like you're Wayne Dyer.

Me: you almost got me. Your opinion used to seem like a fact, little dude. I got worried when you chimed in. no more. I don't believe a word you say. When I hear you speak now, I want to do the opposite of what you say.

Gnome: Oh, so you know everything, huh?

Me: I know the difference between inspiration and fear. Inspiration comes from my Spirit. It makes me come alive. I become enthusiastic. It feels like **living** to me. When you speak, you make me feel afraid. Tense. you make me feel dead. I choose to come alive.

The *between you and me* dialogue, same as the *all about me* offering, lets you receive feedback from your Internal Wisdom.

Use offering #4:

To see from a different perspective.

To solve a problem.

To make a decision.

To make a change.

When you're going through a renewal, for example, a new job or new relationship status.

To forgive yourself.

To forgive someone or something.

hands are for... declaring and deciding

◎ **Decide who you'd like to converse with in a** *between you and me* **dialogue.**

◎ **Choose a topic to journal about in your dialogue. You can review topics and ideas from previous journal entries. Is there anything specific you'd like to change, solve, empower, or forgive?**

◎ **Write the entire journal entry as a dialogue/discussion between your Self and your chosen Interior Voice.**

Here is a list of possible Interior Voices.

Higher Energy or God
Past Self
Child Self
Future Self
Gnome Self (saboteur)
Angel Self (protector, messenger)
Sage Self (wisdom)
Mothering or Fathering Self
Muse

your heart will be persistent
even if you leave it to wither in a shoe box
even if you flatten it and use it as a bookmark to save your place
even if you bury it in the garden between the bossy rows of peppermint
your heart will keep on trying to tell you
what you need to know
to be able to survive
to be able to go on
to rise
to be free.

offering #5

Bruce Springsteen says everybody has a hungry one.

The Hungry Heart exercise

You certainly want to listen to the messages from your heart, because the truth of who you are resides in its energy.

Your heart is hungry for your attention though you'd barely know it. You can hear your mind, no matter what you do. It's a thruway of speeding Corvettes, honking for your attention. Your heart is like the brown Toyota you keep under a tarp in your garage. It was your first car. You've kept your brown car for all these years. It's still reliable. And even though you loved how it made you feel back in the day when you first learned how to drive, you haven't taken it out in a while.

The heart never gets tamed. It doesn't get socialized. And it doesn't forget who you are. The heart carries your pure energy, your pure truth. Your heart is hungry to hit the road. Lift the tarp, raise the garage doors, and drive with your heart. Remember who you are.

Your heart is intuitive and knows your pure desire.
You need only to ask your heart who you are and **trust the answer.**

Use offering #5:

To feel motivated, inspired, or energized.

To make a change.

To forgive yourself.

To forgive someone or something.

To tap into your own wisdom.

To solve a problem.

To make a decision.

When you're going through a renewal, for example, a new job or new relationship status.

hands are for... listening

What does your *Hungry Heart* want to tell you?

Listen to your *Hungry Heart* exercise.
There are <u>two</u> questions for the *Hungry Heart* exercise.
You can journal about each question in the same session or during two separate WiLD sessions.

Sit comfortably in a chair or on the floor. Make sure your back feels relaxed, supported or upright. Place your hands on top of each other over your heart.
Take a few deep, slow breaths.

After 2 minutes of focused, slow breathing ask the first question:

How may I feel of service in my life or how may I feel purposeful?
Repeat the question 3 times. Pause between questions.

Sit in silence. Listen, see, and feel the answer.
The answer usually comes through imagery, from a vision or a feeling.
It usually comes quickly, in a spark or a flash. It might not last.
If you have to wait for a while, you're likely using your mind to notice the answer.
Ask the question again, if you have to. Listen. See. Feel.
The heart is quiet but knowing. It might whisper the answer.

After a few minutes of deep breathing, write what you saw, heard, or felt in your journal.
You can describe your vision/image or you can write the words that encapsulate the
feeling(s). Write your reaction to the image or feeling you received.

Here are a few questions to help you journal about what you saw, heard, or felt when you
listened to your *hungry heart*.

◎ *How may I feel of service in my life or how may I feel purposeful?*
Were you aware of this vision or feeling already? Since when?
Write about other times you felt a similar knowing.
What would make it easier for you to fulfill this service/purpose?
Why would you enjoy moving toward this service/purpose?
Have you ever experienced this feeling or vision in real-life before? Describe.
What needs to happen, change, or what would you need to let go of to live into this service/
purpose?

Marinate on the things you've written for several days. Journal any revelations, changes,
difficulties, or openings that appear as you live and offer your heart to life.

After 2 minutes of focused, slow breathing ask the second question:

How can I show myself love?
Repeat the question 3 times. Pause between questions.
Sit in silence. See, listen, and feel the answer.
Remember, the answer might flash a picture or generate a feeling, so pay attention while breathing slowly.

After a few minutes of deep breathing, write what you saw, heard, or felt in your journal. Describe the vision/picture or write the words that encapsulate the feeling(s). Expand your thoughts.

For the second hungry heart question, consider the following prompts.

○ **How can I show myself love?**
Were you previously aware of the vision or feeling you received?
Are you showing yourself love now? In what ways?
In what ways are you in resistance to showing yourself love? Why?
Have you ever shown yourself love this way? Describe.

During the next few days remain aware of what you've written and felt. Write about any revelations, changes, or difficulties pertaining to the way you show yourself love.

offering #6

conversation starters

Conversation starters (journal prompts) and mind maps (graphic organizers) stimulate ideas, arouse your imagination, and inspire investigation.

Conversation starters are journal prompts. They stimulate thoughts and ideas while *mind-maps* help you organize your thoughts and ideas. You can use both to direct your WiLD when your mind needs guidance.

Mind-maps are commonly used in educational settings to show associations, display comparisons, and break large ideas into smaller chunks. You can journal WiLD about the ideas, thoughts, and outcomes you discover. I prefer to use Venn diagrams, Spider graphs, and T charts.

Venn diagrams compare and contrast ideas. Draw two circles that overlap in the center. The right and left circles represent two subjects or ideas. The overlapping center oval includes the similarities between the right and left subjects. You can overlap three circles to compare three subjects.

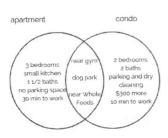

The diagram will highlight journaling topics. For example, you could journal WiLD about the money you'll save if you choose the apartment over the condo, you could write about how you'll use the spare bedroom, or POSSIBILITY journal about living in each of the dwellings until one feels more desirable.

Spider graphs connect ideas, make associations, and expand options. Start by drawing a center bubble. Place a topic, subject, or idea in it. Attach "spider legs" or lines to other bubbles. Place related ideas, thoughts, or options in the attached bubbles.

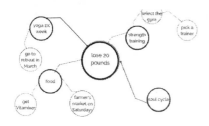

You might journal WiLD about the kind of trainer you want, journal your fears about changing your eating habits, or POSSIBILITY journal about what you'll do when you lose 20 pounds.

T charts compare and contrast two sides of a subject or idea. Each side can represent PROS and CONS, LIKES and DISLIKES, PROFITS and LOSSES, To GO or To STAY, SHORT-TERM and LONG–TERM, and so forth. You can also compare two similar sides like the PROS of two subjects.

Comparing the PROS between a desk job and a private biz

To Stay	To Go
steady salary	double salary/some months
low-cost health benefits	change my work hours/ better for the kids
two co-workers that support me	relocate to a warmer climate

You might journal WiLD about your fear of losing a steady salary, your discipline around doubling your salary, or you might write a POSSIBILITY journal about living in a warmer climate.

Use offering #6:

To feel motivated, inspired, or energized.

To generate or organize ideas.

To make a change.

To see a different perspective.

To forgive yourself.

To forgive someone or something.

To tap into your own wisdom.

To solve a problem.

To make a decision.

When you're going through a renewal, for example, a new job or new relationship status.

hands are for... imagining, listening, and declaring

Here are eight conversation starters, AKA journal prompts, to inspire your entries.
Use any of them as often as you wish to write
a **WiLD Tomato** (for 25 minutes) or a **WiLD Cherry** (for 10 minutes).
Set a soft alarm if you need to stay close to time.

◎ What kind of setting/atmosphere makes you come alive? Describe.
Why?
Consider countries, social settings, events, weather, people.

◎ What's your favorite season? How does it make you feel?
Describe a memory from this season.

◎ Who has given you terrible advice? What did you do with it?
Why was it terrible?

◎ If you could live anywhere for one year, where would it be? Why?
What would you do there? Who would you want with you? How would it change your life?

◎ If someone that previously hurt you told you they were sorry and meant it, how would you
respond? How might it change your life or change your experience with them?

◎ If you could pick anyone alive right now to shadow for a full week, who would it be? Why?

◎ If someone gave you enough money to live for 3 years, what would you do with your life?
Where would you live? How would you spend your time?

◎ What scares you more than anything? Why? Describe.
What if that scary thing could never happen to you?
How would it change your daily life and choices?

the mist can see me through my window. it cannot hide from the glow of the street lamps.

it seems I can't either.

it was raining when the dogs woke up.

it's still raining now.

this is certainly not the way I expected to experience a night in the last days of April:

wrapped in two scarves, socks up my legs, and a fur-lined hat near my front door.

I wanted flowers out my window

and fresh air to blow into my apartment while I readied for bed.

but

I do like the stillness of this night.

I like how time and light hang onto the mist

giving me this evening glow

giving me a slowdown

giving me nowhere to

hide

there is beauty

in this foggy night

offering #7

the awakening

This offering begins with a five to ten minute full-body relaxation (*the awakening*) followed by a 25-minute free-writing session (the WiLD Tomato) or a POSSIBILITY journal entry.

Relaxing with deep breathing centers your energy, letting you imprint a feeling and vision into both your body and subconscious mind (PROGRAM). Your PROGRAM responds to pictures more than words, so you'll need to feel, imagine, and write a journal entry when you practice *the awakening*. Repeat this exercise often and notice how it affects your behavior and your life.

Use offering #7:

To feel motivated, inspired, or energized.

To release energy and heavy psychic weight.

To generate or organize ideas.

To make a change.

To see from a different perspective.

To forgive yourself.

To forgive someone or something.

To tap into your own wisdom.

To solve a problem.

To make a decision.

When you're going through a renewal, for example, a new job or new relationship status.

hands are for... imagining, listening, and deciding

the awakening exercise

The following full-body release lasts for five minutes. You can extend it by maintaining stillness and silence for an five extra minutes.

Before beginning the full-body relaxation,
<u>decide if you will write a WiLD entry or a POSSIBILITY journal entry.</u>

Next, <u>consider a question you want to ponder, an idea you want to examine, or an outcome you desire in your life.</u>
You can select a question or outcome related to your *5 parts of being,* if you want.

◎**Write the question, idea, or desired outcome in your journal.** Read it several times.

The PROGRAM, your subconscious mind, will ponder the question, idea, or outcome while you relax.

Full-Body Relaxation

Set a soft sounding alarm for five or ten minutes on your phone, computer, or use Alexa.
Sit in a comfortable chair or relax on your back. If you choose a chair, it can be a padded chair or a recliner. You do not have to sit upright, but your back needs to feel comfortable.
Make sure your head and neck are relaxed.

Place a palm over your heart and belly, or both palms over your navel or hips, or place your hands six to eight inches away from your sides, palms up.
Begin to notice your breathing. Without trying to control it, allow your breath to flow slowly.
Inhale, and slowly exhale.

As you breathe slowly, relax your feet. Relax your legs. Relax your hips and lower back.

Relax your hands. Relax your arms and shoulders. Soften your mouth. Feel your eyelids soften. Continue breathing slowly until five to ten minutes elapse.
At the sound of the soothing alarm, wiggle your fingers and toes, then stretch your arms over your head gently. Take another deep breath, then exhale. Turn off the alarm.

◎ **Practice a WiLD Tomato or POSSIBILITY journal using the question, idea, or outcome you wrote in your journal. Set another soft-alarm for 25 minutes, if you'd like.**

I encourage you to re-read *the awakening* entries once or twice within the same month they're written. I also encourage you to repeat the exercise with the same or similar question. Whenever you are journaling to listen for an answer or when you want to empower POSSIBILITY, repetition is your magic wand. The more you impress upon your PROGRAM the pictures and images of experiences you desire, the more those impressions affect your behavior and position you to receive your desired outcome.

Our truest life is when we are in dreams awake.

HENRY DAVID THOREAU

claim your page.

Great prophets and scribes etched one brave feat into stone, tablet, and paper.
They wrote: Know thyself.

This is the way to fulfillment.

When you know yourself, you trust your instincts and follow your curiosities. When you know yourself, you feel compelled to live from your truth. When you know yourself you can catch patterns of thinking that have affected you negatively in the past and reroute yourself away from Mundane Junction. When you know your mind, you understand that you can move toward a desired outcome by imagining it *regularly and often.*

Knowing yourself is an ongoing expedition. It requires a commitment to a WiLD ritual. It requires a pen, lips, or fingers that speak. So, pull up a seat, make yourself a journal sandwich, and take a bite out of it every day. Be curious and honest. Use your Voice. Claim your page.

You are about to bond with the greatest person in your life: YOU. You will trust yourself more than you trust anyone else as you endeavor to journal, live, and grow beyond words. Experience everything that you are with your journal, okay? There's a gift in it.

This is a nudge: Listen to your life. Declare your truth. This is a divine wink: You hold your happiness in your hands. This is a call to journal.

Mastering others is strength;
Mastering yourself is true power.

LAO TZU, Chinese Taoist Philosopher

the expedition.

I have created a few more ways ~~to get you as hooked on journaling as I am~~ to help you experience your own transformation by journaling WiLD. First, is the beyond words *realness expedition*. It's a 21-day online journaling course. We'll focus on two goals related to your *5 parts of being*: Finance, Career, Health, Relationship, and Spirituality. You will notice a positive change in the way you think, act, and feel about your specific goals by the end of *the realness expedition* course.

The realness expedition includes three weekly ebooks with instructional videos, audios, and exercises. I'll teach you how to journal WiLD using the seven offerings as well as the **WiLD Tomato** and **WiLD Cherry**. The *realness expedition* will inspire you to take action toward bringing two of your personal goals into real-life.

You'll be able to practice the *beyond words realness expedition* course anywhere—by fireside in a ski resort, from your beach chair in the early sun, or from your window seat at your favorite cafe; wherever you have access to wifi, your journal, and your favorite writing tools.

Second is the complementary journal to *beyond words*: *in your hands—28 days to connect with your Voice, expand your possibilities, and live above ordinary.* Use this journal to deepen your self-awareness, overcome misguiding thoughts and beliefs about yourself, and get on path toward the life you desire.

I've also created a course called *JoG to weight-loss and never look back*. This course is based on my book, *JoG—LOSE WEIGHT, KEEP IT OFF, and NEVER LOOK BACK—this ain't no book about runnin'*. Really. It's not. It's a 9-week transformation from the inside out. In this course you'll identify as a person who believes weight-loss is your right, you'll lose 5-15 lbs, and you'll keep them lost. This course is structured around journaling, tracking your lifestyle, and changing your beliefs about what's possible for you to gain! Expect to improve your relationship with food and your body so you can maintain your success for the long-run.

Knowing thyself is the key to lasting change of any kind. You can inquire about these courses, including the Live Above Ordinary realness community, at www.liveaboveordinary.com/courses .

One more thing. Visit www.liveaboveordinary.com/gift for an **audio journal** focused on weight-loss or stress relief—my gifts to you. Start your most sacred journey with a click and a set of headphones.

Till we meet again, which I hope is soon, may journaling WiLD lead you to live consciously, choose purposefully, and hope limitlessly.

Your imagination can penetrate life.
Michelle Bernard

about the author.

Michelle Bernard spends her days strengthening bodies and elevating minds.

She's a fitness and wellness educator, artist, and pollinator of energy everywhere she roams.

She doesn't mind clay under her nails or a heavy barbell in her hands. Michelle feels magical when applying red lipstick and after soaking in a tub of salt water and essential oil.

She's been in warrior training for many years, though she's only recently realized how to use her power.

For Michelle, life would be incomplete without a corner cafe and her journal. She's always gathering stories. She'd like to hear yours and is willing to share. Meet her on MacDougal in The Village and she'll let you peek into her life-book.

Or at least she'd love to chat with you for hours over a coffee—or seven.

acknowledgements.

Lindamichellebaron, you inspired me, beyond words, when you presented *The Sun is On* poetry to my drama class. When you visited my junior high school, I'm sure you had no idea I was watching closely, listening deeply, memorizing you, and hoping to be free like you someday. This is someday. Thanks for bringing your wild to Iowa. You give magic to children.

Natalie Marie Collins you lit me up during the last stretch of this book. You push me without pushing, and you show the way forward by empowering the steps I naturally take. Your soft strength is full of power. It sparked my spirit and charged me to the finish-line of several projects. You are a lady of light.

A succession of hugs to you, Carolyn LaMargo, for listening to me read pieces of this manuscript in its early stages. You made sure this book wasn't boring. I can't stand boring. You're a soul who goes above and beyond to make me (and everybody) feel better. It worked. You gave much more than I asked for or expected. I treasure you. You radiate love.

Lauren Juceam, I surely miss our nightly calls. I cherish those weekends and summers we spent listening to our hearts, putting our dream bubbles into orbit, and preparing for take-off. I will never forget the night you showed me the SARK-style journal you made in college. The day we did our Shakti Gawain declaration journal at the diner changed my life. Our juicy pens have written us into such succulent outcomes. We've become who we said we'd be, so let's keep on writing our lives.

174

To Noelle Barnard, my sistah in the West who is sharing a creative journey with me: I've taken your advice to make my journal pages wider! I'm still inspired that your hubby described you in his journal before he met you. "More of everything..." That's right, girl.

My dear confidant, Donna Fullerton, thank you for being a human container and carefully holding the words from my heart. Your sweet soul showed up as surprise support while writing this book.

To Buunni Coffee in Riverdale, NY and Max Cafe in Manhattan: you not only gave me an outlet to charge my Mac, you supplied a warm seat, hot drink, and a playlist from the 70's and 80's (yes!). I now enjoy oat milk drinks since trying them the day I capped out on Americanos. Thank you for kindness every time I walked through your door. What barista would say, *Oh, this is your seat* to a customer (me), then get up, and finish her lunch break in another seat? The girl at Max. Exquisite.

For my ladies who journal: Max, Johanna, Carolyn, Celina, and Melissa. Thanks for providing a snippet from your private books for the journal, *in your hands—28 days to connect with your Voice, expand your possibilities, and live above ordinary*. I appreciate you. You are amazing women.

And Mom, thanks for helping me lift the dream I've been writing in my POSSIBILITY journal for the last two years into the stars this year—another chrysalis moment. Love you, butterfly. Biz.

further inquiry.

The SARK books that inspired me most. SARK's journals nudged me to follow my bliss.

Succulent Wild Woman

The Bodacious Book of Succulence

Transformation Soup

Inspiration Sandwich

Julie Cameron, The Voice that lead every artist to get a journal in 1995.

The Artist's Way

Wayne Dyer, you had me at *Real Magic* on cassette in 1995.

The Power of Intention

Wishes Fulfilled

Joe Dispenza keeps breaking paradigms and blowing our minds with his research.

Breaking the Habit of Being Yourself

And at last, the classic:

As A Man Thinketh

James Allen

This is a book about EVERYTHING. You can finish it in a night or two, but you'll *want* to read it again.

This online writing workshop from Andrea Balt and Tyler Knott Gregson rocked.

Write Yourself Alive

There's no limit to how much you'll know,
depending how far beyond zebra you go.

DR. SUESS